A Voice in the Stillness

Slowing Down and Listening Up

Liane,

"Be strong and stable in what it is that you are wanting in life"

σ

[signature]

 FriesenPress

Suite 300 - 990 Fort St
Victoria, BC, V8V 3K2
Canada

www.friesenpress.com

ISBN

978-1-5255-8415-2 (Hardcover)
978-1-5255-8416-9 (Paperback)
978-1-5255-8417-6 (eBook)

1. SELF-HELP, PERSONAL GROWTH, HAPPINESS

Distributed to the trade by The Ingram Book Company

Table of Contents

*May what you need to hear be
the author of my words*

Putting Pen to Paper
(An Introduction)

While some of the finer details may differ, my story is your story

L isten.

Rarely does life give us a chance to take a breath: to do some sorting out, cleaning up, and clearing out.

It's a story that we all know far too well. We get caught up in things. We get too busy.

We lose our sense of equilibrium.

And I was living in that space, for far too long.

So when I was given some unexpected time to find a way back to myself, I took full advantage of it.

These pages hold an account of my journey of letting go, and learning to listen; they speak to all the things I heard in the simplicity of stillness.

There were various paths I took to get there: I started taking stock of the music I was listening to, the things I had been journaling. I paid more attention to what I saw and heard in the world around me.

Step by step, I de-cluttered my mind. I purged my house. I took chances to get away so I would see things from a different vantage point. I did things slightly out of my comfort zone, like a yoga teacher certification. I started meditating more frequently. And I did all of these things because I just *knew* I had to do them.

Yes, it was like I unknowingly took the equilibrium I had lost and I shook it even more. And I found myself on very unfamiliar ground.

But I settled into it, because it felt just right: because it was, in fact, *solid* ground.

And as time went on, I started listening more, hearing more, and writing more. The act of putting pen to paper became my primary source of connecting to something higher than myself but it also came from listening to and observing the world around me. And much came from conversations with the dear friends and family members who make up my 'cloud of witnesses'.

Divinity is alive and well. It is all around us: always and in all ways.

And it is available to us all.

We all have had those moments of awe when we just *know* that something is happening that is 'other worldly'.

Like when someone dies and we feel like the rug has been pulled out from under us, and we gain the strength and courage to continue moving forward.

Or, when we hold a baby in our arms and have that feeling of inexplicable joy.

There is an awareness—in these moments—that there is something going on that is much deeper.

This is the part of the story that many of us keep in the deep recesses of our minds.

But this is the story that I choose to tell.

So, I bare my heart to you in these pages, with these words.

Be kind with them because when I share with you my story, I also share with you my vulnerability. I write about my inner dialogue—the private thoughts that swim around in my mind—and the truths that I desperately needed to hear.

And I share this with you because, in this world of individuality, we are all much more deeply interconnected than we would like to think. While some of the finer details may differ, my story is your story, and your friend's story, and your friend's, friend's story.

We all have a past that we carry with us in varying degrees. We all try to live in the present moment. We all look ahead to the future with wavering emotion.

It is my hope that many of the words on these pages will remind you of what you have forgotten, show you things you need to see, and give you the words you need to hear.

There may be truths so plainly black and white that they bring you to tears. At times, they may prove to be a mirror that you do not want to see.

So, this book isn't for the faint of heart.

But it has found its way to you. Perhaps it has been written with the divine's eye right on you.

Either way, always remember that these words are written in love.

Listen...

Lost and Found

That jar of hope in my heart was filling up

This is not a light-hearted backstory.

I could start by talking about how I moved out when I was 16 years old. I could tell you about getting hit by a drunk driver in my twenties, who left me for dead, broke more bones in my body than I care to remember, and how I had to re-learn how to walk. I could tell you countless other stories of where life seemed to have taken me on a wrong turn, but I won't.

I say these things so you know some of the things that have shaped the person I am today.

So, fast-forward the clock to a few years later. Things are looking pretty good: I've been married for a good while. I have a house, a car, and a really good job. And I find out that I'm expecting!

I really don't think anyone can truly explain how good it feels to have a miracle growing inside you. For me, I sang songs with more passion, I smiled a little bigger, it was like I had little butterflies in my belly and my heart was just that little bit lighter.

My belly started growing, and we shared our news, and everyone was just that little bit nicer.

And it was awesome.

Until we found out halfway through that something was wrong. We went for tests, and then more tests, and the hours and minutes that passed went excruciatingly slowly as we waited by the telephone, as we set up new appointments, as we prayed, and as we just waited...

But then we found ourselves in the delivery room, labouring through to an inevitable outcome.

And she was gone before she was ever really with us.

*

A little over a year later, our lovely little Naomi came into this world. And while we felt like we were holding our breath throughout the entire pregnancy, while we prayed constantly for peace of mind—that was always laced with trepidation—that beautiful miracle of a girl came to us.

And how we love her, and want the very best for her.

Which is why I had it on my heart to have another child. I just knew in my heart of hearts that another child was meant for us. But with everything we had been through with our first, and the fear that my husband went through during the second pregnancy, he was not prepared to have another.

After many attempts to persuade him otherwise, we agreed on adoption and away he went for a vasectomy (whether I agreed to this or not).

And then he wasn't so sure about the adoption.

I felt nothing less than betrayed.

So then came years of hoping and praying—of begging and pleading—that he would change his mind, or that I would get pregnant despite the odds. These prayers, layered also with grief from the loss of our first.

And as the months went by, that little jar of hope in my heart was emptying. The distance between us grew wider. And I threw myself into my work, and that seemed to keep my mind elsewhere.

Then my Nanny (my maternal grandmother) who meant more to me than any other adult in the world, got sick and went into palliative care. I jumped on a plane as fast as I could get there. I flew into her room and took her hand in mine and brought it to my cheek before anyone had the chance to tell me that touching her would cause her agonizing pain. And then she was gone.

Of all the love she gave me in my life, my last moment with her caused her pain.

So, I picked up my laptop and started working on the eulogy; this was something I had some semblance of control over.

Through tear-filled conversations, I gathered together the most precious stories of her life, her love for others, and her faith.

The day of the funeral, I walked into the church and sat in a pew. It didn't take long before I was sobbing, so much that I started to worry whether I would be able to get through it all.

And then, I pulled myself together. I tucked away my grief. I put the thoughts that were swimming in my mind on pause and walked up to the lectern. There I was, standing in front of a microphone, speaking words that were meant to bring some comfort to us all:

"And oh, if we could capture that knowledge, that wisdom, that advice, and all of those memories in a jar, how lovely it would be! To be able to just slightly open the jar up and know what she would say, and hear that lovely voice of hers..."

I shared a poem I had written about her years and years earlier:

Petals from roses and soft silky towels,
Warm hugs and kisses and baking for hours,
This is what she is to me.
The clinking of a spoon on the side of a cup,
The smell of fresh bread in the morn' when I
get up,
Are all sweet reminders to me.
Her tenderness, care, her sweetness and giving,
Her sheer love of life, her wisdom, forgiving.
These are the things that I see in her eyes.
This angel, a wife, a mother, a Nan,
Is perfectly gentle and more precious than a
priceless gem...
And she holds the key to my heart.

And then I folded up those written words, packed up my suit-case, and flew back home the very next day. I recall getting on the plane, putting on my headphones, and starting a sad movie so I wouldn't have any onlookers: I cried all the way home.

We all grieve in our own way.

And then I was back at work. I would take moments, as fleet-ing as they were—mostly in the car—to have a tearful break-down, and life went on.

But my heart was broken.

In fact, quite literally—I found out a few months after that my heart was indeed broken—I needed heart surgery—I was a walking time bomb.

So, I sat down and had the discussions no one wants to have regarding wills, and raising our child, and all that morbid stuff no one in their thirties wants to be thinking about.

But I was ready, because I had shut down. I was angry. I was alone. And I had lost any ounce of hope I had left in me.

And into the hospital I went. Into a surgery that still gives me nightmares. And while I lay there, I thought about my life. What a mess I've made of it. And I've lost a little girl. And I've lost the only person in the world who I felt ever *really* loved me. And I've lost hope.

Please take me now...

But my story wasn't over. They put a fix on my heart. So, back home I went, and lying on the couch, still recovering from a broken heart, not even sure what step to take next, my husband Gareth walks in.

He walks in with a paper in his hand of a little girl with long black hair who is up for adoption. Gareth: the one who at one point wasn't ready to adopt; the one who a precious friend prayed for, that he would be able to visualize what he wanted his family to look like; the one who 'betrayed' me, but who now was ready and had found a way to try to make it up to me.

I quickly told myself that this little girl had far too many other families interested in adopting her. I tried not to read too much into the fact that Naomi took one look at the picture of this little girl and replied emphatically, *"that's* my little sister!" I tried to keep restrained when we were short-listed to go in for an interview, but I soon realized that I was setting myself up for a possible fall because that jar of hope in my heart was filling up.

And I wanted this so badly.

So fast-forward just a short while later. The hours and minutes that passed went excruciatingly slowly as we waited by the telephone. And we prayed. And we waited. And then came the call: *we* were chosen to adopt this little girl. Us!

And we knew it was right. We could feel it in every ounce of our being.

We knew it even before she moved in, when a friend we hadn't seen for a while came up to me asking if she had missed something because she was sure she had seen us the week before with a little girl with long black hair.

We knew it the first night she slept over when we tucked her in and her chosen bedtime song was, the "I Love You Song"[1].

And we knew it when we looked up the meaning of this little girl's name—Desi:

So long hoped for...

What was lost had now been found.

So, this is my story. It is the story of how I had given up, and how 'my tomb' was opened, and how my despair was replaced with blessings, with light, with love, far greater than I could have ever hoped for.

Master of Disguise

But then, before you know it, it loses its allure

Perhaps I was destined to be a little eclectic in my thinking about what a spiritual journey could look like...

My Nanny was a Pentecostal, and my earliest days were spent in a highly experiential sanctuary with lively, emotive behaviours: traditional gospel-choir singing, arm-raised 'hallelujahs', and born-again freedoms filled the room. Hugging, laughing and holding hands were unspoken rites and even as a little child, I could tell that these church doors were welcome to anyone. This is where I heard songs that had lovely imagery and were beautifully inclusive like, "This Little Light of Mine"[2], and "Jesus loves the little Children"[3].

My father, and his very large family, grew up as devout Roman Catholics. So, when I was around 8 years old, two decisions were made: first, I stopped going to Pentecostal church and second, I switched from the public-school system to the Canadian separate school board to get a Catholic education. I 'caught up' by receiving my First Holy Communion a year late. To encourage me to get up to speed, my godmother recorded some of the main prayers and creeds. From then on, I was on the 'normal' Roman Catholic path and attended weekly Sunday mass.

Mass was a stark contrast to my previous experience. There were many things to learn that I was quite unaccustomed to: there was a specifically acceptable way to dip your finger in the holy water and to make the sign of the cross. You needed to genuflect before you entered the pew. There were many other rules to learn, and since there was no Sunday School in the early years, my primary focus was twofold. First, I tried my very best not to do anything to get in trouble: this was church and you *never* misbehaved. As an extension of this, the second thing that occupied my time was to focus on mastering my knowledge of when to sit, kneel, genuflect, and where to follow in the hymnal and the missal.

Over time, this grew to me noticing people who *didn't* know these rituals. I admittedly took some secret pleasure in their lack-of-knowing, mostly because it highlighted to me my A+ knowledge in this area. Either way, it made me stand a tad taller and take some pride in my accomplishments. The slight over-achiever that I tend to be, I then set myself a new goal of learning grand portions of the Eucharistic prayer and pre-communion rites. I almost effortlessly spoke them under my breath with the priest each Sunday.

While this might sound entirely torturous to some, it taught me very good discipline. Also, it provided me with the skill of finding the silver lining in the 'cloud' of sometimes-didactic church teaching. I learned to focus on the gold nuggets in the homily and take pleasure in the moments when we could participate, like singing. I learned songs that still give me chills to this day. Songs like, "Eagle's Wings"[4], "Be Not Afraid"[5], and "Here I am, Lord"[6].

And, while some people take great pleasure in knowing that no matter where they go, they can step into a Roman Catholic church and find a constant there—a ritual that is familiar, and purely comforting—for me, reciting the exact words over and over can make them lose their meaning over time. The power behind the words can diminish.

It's like a song that stops you in your tracks, brings you to tears, or gives you head-to-toe goose bumps. You hear the song and then you can't stop replaying it until you know every word, every pause, and every intonation. You want to take in every bit of joy and happiness it can give you.

But then, before you know it, it loses its allure. And then another song comes along with a similar uplifting theme, and you take great pleasure in singing the words in a different way to bring you a newly found joy.

This is human nature.

Now, this is not to say that we should throw out the old and constantly strive for something shiny and new. But rather, it is to say that keeping things alive—and moving—sometimes means seeing them from another perspective. Seeing things from a slightly different angle challenges us to re-learn, to refresh, to re-see, to remember.

Be open-minded to such things. 'Different' doesn't always mean 'alien', or 'wrong'. And we don't want to keep ourselves so shrouded in what we are accustomed to that we dampen the spark altogether; we don't want the need for mere familiarity to mask our ability to grow.

God is a beautiful master of disguise. He will gently find his way to you in numerous ways, if you are open to it.

It is simply like clothing that comes in and out of style—all of it is merely material that we put on to cover our bodies. It may come in different forms, colours, patterns, or styles, but in the end, it's all the same:

The truth is the truth.

The Beginning
of the Beginning

*Life often takes little turns and changes its course
in many seemingly insignificant ways*

You never know when your life is going to take a turn and change its course entirely.

I'm driving home in cats-and-dogs rain. The kind of rain where you have to drive lower than the speed limit with your windshield wipers on max, and you can still hardly see a thing.

And I'm processing what just happened. It's 9:30 a.m., a little early to be doing my commute home already. I look down at the envelope with the details of my package inside. I'm replaying what happened in my mind: the people I saw when I was being walked out, the discussions that happened in the HR room about making my job redundant. The consultant who admitted that I didn't look too shocked about the whole thing.

A thousand thoughts flood in, almost instantaneously, fighting for my attention:

I wonder when this started? Good thing I talked to Gareth last week and said I had a feeling that I was going to lose my job. Ha! Women's intuition—it's always right! I wonder who will be leading the 10:30 meeting? I guess those emails in my inbox don't matter now. Man, it feels good to have nothing due. Was it something I did? Isn't this weather so typical? Is it ominous that I am not more upset about this? Don't take it personally. You just got a get-out-of-jail-free card! Gareth's at home—so interesting, since he is never home during the day: he works outdoors, and trudges through most weather, but he would never work in this downpour. Good. We'll have a chance to chat about how to tell our kids, so they aren't concerned. I wonder how my team at work will react? They're likely being told now. I think I kind of asked for this.

And then I turn on the radio. It seemed like it was waiting in queue for me to turn it on. The chorus of "Big Girls Don't Cry"[7] blared out of my speakers.

Damn Fergie, that's right on point.

So, off went the radio and in came the relief. I just breathed in the joy, the freedom, and the satisfaction. It washed over me. Because without knowing how or why, there was clear acknowledgement of the perfect timing of it all. The rain and the dark skies may have tried, but they weren't able to shroud the gleaming light in my heart.

And over the next little while, I came to better understand why.

Because, while this day might have been a monumental one it wasn't the true beginning of a new beginning. I think we often think that one thing happens and it changes our life forever. But things in life typically don't just happen in one fleeting moment.

The 'beginning' starts much earlier than this.

Life often takes little turns and changes its course in many seemingly insignificant ways. And it is the sum of all of these little changes, the little wishes you send out, the gut-wrenching knowing that something is wrong, the desperate prayers you say, the songs that you sing at the top of your lungs, etc., that can end up changing the course of your life entirely.

So after I sorted out some of the financial details, one of the first things I did was to go through my favourite playlist and look at the lyrics of all the songs that I'd been listening to. I paid special attention to the songs that I sang from my heart of hearts and the depths of my diaphragm, the ones that brought tears to my eyes, or elicited other deep emotions.

While this exercise took a lot of time (it was a great, but long, playlist), it didn't take long for me to gain some insight into the energy that I was 'putting out there'.

I had been screaming to the universe my unconventional prayers. The themes looked something like this:

Feeling lost and/or wanting to hide:

> Don't cry for me Argentina: Madonna[8]
> Iris: Goo Goo Dolls[9]
> Why: Annie Lennox[10]
> Hello: Adele[11]
> Fight Song: Rachel Platten[12]

Questioning what all the striving is for:

> Reaching: Ali Matthews[13]
> All of my Life: Phil Collins[14]
> Try: Colbie Caillat[15]

Desperate pleas to make it stop:

> Breakdown: Jack Johnson[16]
> Walk Away: Christina Aguilera[17]
> River: Sarah McLachlan[18]

A touch of hope and wishful thinking that things would get better:

Come by the Hills: Loreena McKennitt[19]
Hold On: Wilson Phillips[20]
Rainbow: Kesha[21]
I'll be: Edwin Cole McCain[22]
Man in the mirror: Michael Jackson[23]

The words to these songs were like a smack in the face and a celebratory high-five all at the same time.

And then I took a look at the songs I was drawn to learn on the guitar. There were similar themes:

Something is not quite right:

Landslide: Dixie Chicks version[24]
Blackbird: Sarah McLachlan version[25]

Time is ticking:

Wake me up: Avicii[26]
I will remember you: Sarah McLachlan version[27]
American Honey: Lady Antebellum[28]

Keep an eye on the lyrics you listen to, as well as the books that come your way, the people you spend time with, the things you hang on your walls, the movies you watch, the things that generate a spark of 'something' in you. There's likely something you need to hear. There's likely something your inner child is crying out for, if you listen closely enough.

But even more blatant than anything else in that playlist was a song by Daughter[29]. I was infatuated with the song since I first heard it in a hot yin yoga class. I played the song incessantly, and it encapsulated it all: life was wearing me down and I needed a fresh start.

The song was called, "Medicine". Considering that much of my career was in the pharmaceutical industry, the song was like a diagnosis, and the lyrics were like a salve for my soul.

*

My *heart's desires* were unequivocal: I had almost been pleading for something like this to happen.

After that, I read through my journals. If you're not someone who writes down your thoughts, consider it, even if it's infrequently. I used to write in a journal only once every 18 months or so when I was able to get away on a weekend women's retreat. Typically, I would be completely antisocial and isolate myself by finding a secluded place. Before I would start writing, I would read my previous journal entries. Often, I would notice how many of the exact same things were still running around in my head. This sometimes gave me the kick in the pants I needed to start doing something about it, because there is power in seeing something clearly written—more than once —in black and white.

And in the writing, the signs of unspoken dreams are often there, but sometimes you can't see them until the time is right.

Sometimes you're blinded to the signs because other things stand in the way of them, or perhaps you don't *want* to see them. For me, I wouldn't allow myself to see the signs because they made no logical sense to me whatsoever: I absolutely LOVED the type of work that I did. I was in a senior leadership position building programs to help patients to navigate through the gaps and barriers in the Canadian reimbursement and healthcare systems. I had almost two decades of experience doing this. It challenged me on a daily basis. I led ethics-based workshops and was able to participate in discussions and decision-making on very complex issues. I never knew what my day would look like, and I thrived in this environment. I took pride in my work. I had status. It would have been foolish to just walk away from such a thing.

So, I gave the job my all.

And, if I wanted to do something new and exciting, I simply found a way to 'fit it in' to my schedule. A couple of years earlier, I had added a big thing to my roster of activities: I signed up to finally do the master's degree that I had carved in my heart over 20 years prior.

I fast-tracked through the full-time degree, on top of full-time work, and a busy home life with two growing girls under the age of 10.

I know. What was I thinking?

Despite that—but by the grace of God—I landed on the Dean's Honour List, awarded to the top 10% of the graduating class.

If I'm going to do something, I'm going to do it right—even if it comes close to killing me.

That, or God needed me to stop telling myself the lie that I picked up somewhere along the way that I was stupid.

But then, since completing the degree, I struggled to come down from the fast-paced life I had become accustomed to. I took a course in Huna meditation to help. I went to hot yin yoga classes to try to slow down. But I was still tired and I didn't feel like I had a way out. So, because there was no point in wallowing in it, I just trudged on as well as I could.

So fast-forward to after the job was done. I re-read my journal entries and it was only then that I could clearly see what my journal entries were cautioning me over a year earlier. The words were stuck in between a deluge of other stream-of-consciousness entries that made the warning signs harder to see at the time. They weren't in plain view, until now:

"Maybe it's time for a change. I can feel a big change coming." (July)

"I feel a change is brewing, but it will be a good one!" (Aug)

"My mind is tired. I'm drained. Maybe it means that my passion for this is subsiding. Time to move on?" (Sept)

"I think I'm getting lost in the shuffle of busyness." (Sept)

Well, there you go.

No wonder it wasn't pure shock when it happened. Some would say that I had manifested this without even knowing it.

The journal also helped me to reacquaint myself with some of my wishes, goals, desires, and imaginings. It also reminded me of certain attitudes I had picked up along the way.

So, as I read the entries, I wrote down the hopes and dreams, the reminders of things I knew to be true, and the 'clues'. I wrote them all on little sticky notes and organized them in sections on a large piece of poster board.

And then, while everything was still fresh in my mind, I mapped out the big-picture story of my life on the backside of that board. I wrote out key milestone moments in my life that shaped the person that I am today. Around each milestone event, I added layers of different information.

First, I marked some bullet-point details describing the milestone. Then, I added key songs and quotes that were needed wisdom for me at the time. For example, around one milestone I wrote a section of a Howard Jones' song called "Life in One Day"[30].

All in all, it was a fun walk down memory lane.

But it took a little while to do.

And it was hard because I also jotted down what I *learned* through these milestone moments. While there were many positive things, I also wrote things like, 'I was a shame to my family simply by being born,' 'People can only take me in small doses,' 'I am stupid,' and 'I don't belong.'

Intense stuff.

The map had a big question mark at the end because I wasn't sure where was I headed. So, I looked through my journals again to think about some key things that I had thought of doing for many years like 'get a yoga instructor certification'. And, this specific goal captured my attention. I also added words that described what I loved to do like 'storytelling,' and 'teaching,' and 'travelling.'

The last step in this process was to jot down all of the things that I knew to be true about myself that weren't illusions or lies that I might have talked myself into over the years. I also added things that were empowering, which included compliments that people had given me over the years that I had forgotten— until now.

And with all this in front of me, I was inspired to cut and paste magazine pictures on to a corkboard. I completely re-freshed my inspiration board that visualized what I want my life to be.

It's hung in my closet so I can see it every day.

Next up, I purged my house. For anyone who knows me, the fact that I lasted this long before starting the purge is impressive. Albeit humorous, I would like to look at it like good evidence that I'm growing as a person.

Because the top two floors of our two-storey house were in pretty good shape, it didn't take me too long to do the purge. In

THE BEGINNING OF THE BEGINNING

fact, it would probably be more appropriate to say that it was an exercise in re-acquainting myself with my stuff.

Sometimes when we are so busy, we lose touch with the wonderful memories that surround us in our homes, so doing a little dusting and holding on to some of our sentimental stuff can be cathartic and grounding.

But the basement was an entirely different story. Our home was built in 1880, and has an old rubble basement to prove it. This old part of the house is dusty, and sometimes musty, and often cobweb-y. Although we use it mostly as a storage room, it's also where we bring things to die: old tables, lamps, and things we just don't have a place for often make their way to this room, never to return.

Although I pass by the door to this room every time I go down my basement stairs, it is one room that I don't visit often; the room is almost analogous to the shadows tucked away in my mind. It's also where our furnace, cistern, sump pump, and water heater are found. So, I left it for my husband to contend with.

And my husband's office is the next room I see. On a clean and organized scale, I likely rank an 8 or a 9 (some people might say an 11). My husband on the other hand, would likely rank a 2 or a 3. But it's his room and I've been given strict instructions not to touch it.

The girls have to pass through this disorganized-looking den to get in to their playroom, so I often imagine the girls turning on their 'it's ok for us to make a mess' switch as they walk by to play with their toys. This should give you an indication of the state of affairs in the playroom as I walked in to start the clearing process.

So over 50 hours later, my purge of that room—and the storage room next to it—was complete.

25

You may question how it took me over 50 hours, but this exercise had very good parts to it. It included getting rid of a ton of books and stuff I had been holding on to that no longer served me. It gave me the chance to organize our photo boxes. It also included going through my special-memories box, and pulling out things that I have intentionally held on to for almost 30 years.

And my girls were able to see my old sketches from high school, and play with my collection of toy figurines I got from a popular fast food restaurant in the late 80s. I was able to reminisce about so many great memories. I found things I had saved from my grade 8 class (which was my hardest, but my favourite year of school). I was also able to reconnect with a friend I had met in the summer between grade 11 and 12 when we went on a six-week bursary program in northern Quebec.

All in all, these hermit-like exercises gave me a chance to feel more grounded: I had reconnected with my home, but more importantly, I had started reuniting with parts of me that I had lost.

This was my formal 'beginning of the beginning' of the process of remembering what I had forgotten.

Ray of Sunshine

Stand strong and shine brightly

Around the time of the journal review, and the purging, I did take *some* time to be social: I met for leisurely lunches with friends and family. One friend of mine was able to validate my thinking that going away—anywhere—was a wise choice.

Having some time on your own is so important because our identity can take on the roles of wife, Mom, sister, daughter, and friend, and this can cloud your mind; it can keep you busy enough that you forget the depth of who you are.

So a few days later, while driving, I had a thought that flashed into my mind, as clear as day. But—at the same time—it made no sense to me at all. Call it a hunch, but I instantly knew that I needed to go out west to see a cousin, visit with an acquaintance (who I hardly knew) and go to spend some time with relatives I had just met the summer before.

Random.

So I reached out to each of them, and they were all elated over the idea. They all said that the timing was *perfect* and I didn't know how much *they* needed this.

And here I thought that this trip was all about me.

I did only preliminary planning to stay with each of them. Other than the times of my flights, I had no set agenda. I may have been sleeping on a couch, but none of that mattered.

To be clear, this type of thing was very foreign to me; it wasn't something that I did. I didn't like putting anyone out so I would typically stay in a hotel or a bed and breakfast even when visiting family.

That said, here I was doing some very loose preparations for a trip out west. Going into the unknown, to spend time with people that—in the grand scheme of things—I hardly knew.

But I just *knew* that I had to go. I could feel it in my bones.

And as chance would have it, I had enough points to cover the entire trip.

And then, there I was, in unfamiliar territory.

And two thirds of my time away was filled with me listening. Everyone kept telling me how much I was giving them, but I felt like I was receiving so very much more: when you give you receive[31].

And as I say this, the crown of my head feels like a ray of sunshine is beaming down on me.

We all have experiences like this. But sometimes we don't listen to what our heart peacefully knows is true, because we can't make any sense of it.

But the wisdom of knowing something—with a peace attached to it, without being able to explain it logically—is often *how* you know it's truth.

In this case, I just *knew* that out west was exactly where I needed to be.

When you're open to give love, and when you're equally open to receive love, that's where the 'magic' happens:

After days of listening and open-heartedness, some deep-rooted questions started gently popping into my mind.

Most of them were unspoken, tucked safely inside my head. Some were mere whispers that indirectly planted themselves into conversation.

None of the questions were laced with worry or distress: they were simple inquiries, sheer curiosity: what are the skills that I bring in to this world that would be of *value*? How do I deal with other people's negative energy? Why do I not feel connected with everyone? What does the future hold?

So, by approaching each moment with intrigue, and a welcoming in of the joyful unknown—by staying light and buoyant in conversation—I called divinity in, and my questions, one by one, started getting answered.

This is what I heard:

The natural state of being of all who are incarnate is one where you are all at peace, where you are all filled with joy, and light, and love, and goodness, and kindness, and compassion. Many of these are mentioned in the bible as the fruit of the spirit[32].

Now, you are very good at transmuting negative energies; you have been given a gift where you can take people's 'worldly' energy—the different vibrations that trouble those who are incarnate on this planet—and put it through to them, add to them that which is needed, for them to be restored.

You uplift them.

It is not that you are necessarily doing anything that is airy, fairy, or magic, or mystical. When someone is feeling uncomfortable, you are simply able to detach from what they are experiencing and allow them to experience those emotions without there being any judgment or shaming. Then, you are able to return the energy back to them in a new form; you mirror back to them their natural state of being.

For example, your home is a house that is filled with love, but it is also a house that is in the world. And your young ones come to you, and find their strength and security within you, the parent. You do not necessarily transmute their negative energy in word, but in vibration: you do it through the kindness, and the gentleness, and the love that you extend to them.

You take their angst, fear, worry, and upset—the things that weigh people down—and help them to return to a 'higher' state of buoyancy, light-heartedness, and the fullness of life.

The reason why you are able to do this is because you yourself are standing in the presence of love. *This* is your natural state of being. And because you are filled with love for these ones, you are able to stand there, and let the storm come, because you are standing straight and tall.

So, it is not that you are removing anything, but rather you are just allowing yourself to be in the world, but not of the world. You are permitting yourself to be in their world—and not of their world—for the storm is not necessarily going on around you, but rather it is swirling around them. You give them the strength, the certainty, and the love, that allows them to be able to be calm and at peace once again.

And this isn't just something that is unique in you. You *all* have the capacity to access this. It is the natural state of all who are incarnate.

Now this can happen with many, for there are those that one would call the prickly pears in your life. You are able to allow them to be who they are, and then you are able to minister to them, you could say, from a place of stability. This is not meant to necessarily mean the lack of the annoyance, or the irritation, but rather you have the ability to, vibrationally—in the moment—speak clearly to them.

You do not shame them. You do not create the drama—the unnecessary fear-based thinking—the pushing against. This is where they are; it is not your business. You are just there to be the sound post. They may have a different vibration, different beliefs, different thoughts, different stories they are telling, but these stories have no impact on you unless you give them the power.

It is a so what, and it is also what is so.

And you do this when you are grounded: you let the other person be where they are with no need for defence because God is with you. The love is flowing.

There is no need to read into it, and understand what it is and what it isn't.

Ruminating, and assuming is something that you do not need to do. This is the kind of thing that will drain your life in an instant. Remain clear in your own mind with what it is that you are wanting. Because, if there were 12 people in your life, and all of them were pulling you in different directions, what would you do then?

Just get on with what it is that you want to do. And give them the freedom to do what they like to do. Knowing that they have the right to do what they need to do for whatever reason.

Your job is not necessarily to change or shift or manipulate or cajole, but rather to say things like 'well, good luck,' or 'enjoy.' There is nothing lost, you simply say, 'I wish you well.'

And your children learn that it is all right to have people in your life with different opinions and views.

There is an easy phrase to use if you are in the midst of negative energy. For example, if someone is telling you something with their finger wagging, or acting with the 'in your face' business, you can allow them to do this and then look kindly at them and say, 'I am sorry to hear you were offended, that was not my intention. I was merely asking for clarity. Forgive me.'

The situation is diffused in an instant. And you leave it there. They will either say 'yes you are' or 'no you are not' forgiven. But it is at that point that it is not yours anymore. It has been erased.

So, when you have someone who is upset with you, you cannot change what they are experiencing, or thinking, or believing. But what you can do is to remain strong and stable. There is no reason for you to believe that you were the jerk, or the one who was causing deliberate harm, just because they are experiencing it. You look and say 'I'm terribly sorry. It was not my intention to cause you any harm or discomfort. What would you want from me now? What can we do now?'

It diffuses everything.

Where there can be resolving, in such a way, that it benefits all concerned, then so be it. But if a common ground cannot be found, be encouraged, my dear, to not slip into guilt, shame, or blame. All is well.

This is a very important point, for many of you on this planet tend to hold on so tightly with the past. You have a foothold on things—real or imagined—that you believe have occurred that have caused harm or that have irritated and such, that you literally separate yourselves from that which is waiting for you always, which is the guidance and the love.

And you can call upon divinity at any time.

You have come far enough along to know that you merely have to quietly ask for assistance: 'What is it that you would have me do?' And in that stillness of the deep breath—which takes no more than five seconds to do—you will be able to release the tension, and allow the knowledge to be received.

Many people feel a desire, or even pressure, to feel more connected to others, especially to people in close proximity to them.

What gives you the assumption that it should be this way?

There are different levels of vibrational frequency of each one that walks the earth. You will have some people in your life where the energy just simply flows freely—there is no effort there.

You're simply not going to have that with everyone.

There is no reason why you should assume that you will have it with everyone.

Some are more 'worldly' attached than you, and this is ok. This is where they are. You love them where they are. Be at peace with where they are.

But here is the key: you must develop the power, to let go of your judgment that you should have it so. You are all children of the one who created you. And each one, with their different experiences, and different choices that are made through these experiences—out of these—create the basis of their belief system. And the more you think of something, the more you believe it.

And similarly, regarding the relationship with your spouse, you are very good in the connection that the two of you have. But do remember that the world's expectations are quite different for how the male should function than it is for the female.

So, approach your spouse with tolerance, with a little bit of humour, as well as with an understanding that there is a vibration that these ones have to deal with that is far more, let's say, aggressive in nature.

Softly encourage him to be at peace with where he is, as well. For this one is hard on himself at times and there must be the encouragement, and the reminder, that he too, is a bright light, and is the son of the greater God. Remind him that all is well. They respond very well to the encouragement, and to the praise.

And you must always remember that you are all here to experience the deliciousness of life. If you allow the problems of others—or the differences you see between you and those around you—to take that away from you, then it is not yours. You must always make the choice. Do not make the choice to allow other people's storms, or experiences, or dramas, to interfere with your inner peace, with your returning to your natural state of being.

You will find that those of you who have the higher vibration will be drawn to one another. Keep encouraging each other.

You have come a long way my dear. You have lived a life that has been filled with incredible amounts of, let's say, 'opportunities' for you to release your attachment to the body, to the ways of the world, and to the mass consciousness outlook. And yes, it does put you in a place of feeling as though you are 'out of step'.

But, the permanence of the life experience, and society's view is always something that you must take into consideration.

Ten generations from now, there will be a different viewpoint and the perception will change. So, flow, as you have done, dear one.

It matters not what modality you pick up to keep your vibration high, what matters is the ability to release the attachment to the world, and use that modality as a means for you to attune yourself with your natural state of being, which is one of holiness. In the moment that you connect yourself with spirit, it is a holy instant.

For example, you are looking into doing the yoga certification. A yoga that is done without an attunement with—or the ability to connect with—spirit is not a holy experience at all. It would be a yoga that one could be using for all manners of things: 'I *do* yoga,' 'I do *yoga*,' '*I* do yoga.' It can be used to aggrandize oneself. It turns into an ego thing.

This is the cutting through ego-based materialism. It matters not if you have the Reiki or Huna, or the certification in this one, or that one. These are all important tools to be used in the service of humanity, to help others to be able to attune themselves to spirit to see how precious they are, or can be.

So, if you are being called to do this, if you feel that you know in your belly when you hear it, and you think 'I believe this will be helpful', then let me tell you, that indeed it will be.

And what you will receive out of it will be what you are giving into it.

You are one who is very connected to your physical form— this is meant in the positive way—you are able to speak to your body and to hear what it has to say—but remember that you are far greater than physicality; you are spirit incarnate.

And about the future, the greatest thing you can do is to approach it with joyful expectation: 'I wonder what is coming next? I'm so excited. What gifts am I going to use? Where is God going to place me? Where can I be of service?'

Speak as often as you can to the divine spirit in you, but speak with the expectation of joy. Don't try to paint the picture of how it *will* be or how it *should* be. Just listen to your heart. You are very connected to it. Listen to it. Listen to what it is that you are hearing from your non-physical self about the next step.

You are coming into a phase in your life right now, where the authenticity of who you are is going to be utilized more. You are going to allow your natural way of being to come forward. You are going to embrace the wonder and beauty of who you are, as you were created, with more with certainty and with confidence.

You are going to be able to stand strong and shine brightly.

There is one more thing, because it still does trouble you at times, for you are still wanting to have everybody be happy and at peace: you seem to, at times, be the chameleon, and to be what other people want you to be in order for other people to feel comfortable. Stop this!

Stop it immediately.

Do not worry about those around you. They are well. They are fine. They are on their journey. You don't have to be dampening yourself down to be part of the crew. Just listen and encourage people. Let them know that they are far greater than they think they are.

For what is true for you is true for them. They just have not laid down the lies long enough to see it.

There is no ending to this life, so you do not ever get it done because it is never over. So do not be afraid by the fear mongering that goes on around you. Just hold fast to the knowledge that whatever is coming is going to take you on a wonderful journey.

The challenge for you now, is for you to be at peace with where you are, in the lack of busyness.

So as you move forward, remember to speak with gratitude to that small child inside yourself. Look at what you have inside you more than what you do not have.

This doesn't mean that there won't be days when you are miserable, when you are tired and you are hungry. But when you look at yourself in these times, do you see love for self?

If you cannot see it in yourself, you will not be able to give it to others.

So when those fears come, in those dark and cold nights, wrap yourself in a warm blanket, wrap your arms around yourself, and reassure yourself that all is well.

And keep as many positive folks around you and teach them to do the same: those who are willing to be happy, and play, and enjoy life, and see the good things in life. Yes, there are wars. Yes, there are things going on. You cannot physically do anything, but you can pray! You can picture quietly those who are suffering and say, 'Please God, I send all the love I have at this moment, the love you have given me. I ask you to shower it upon them'. There is tremendous power in prayer. You have a tremendous gift in being able to acknowledge that connection.

Shine your light for others.

This is all for now. But in the meantime, write down what you believe your gifts and your talents are. What are the innate vibrations that flow through you easily—that light you up naturally—that you find to be exceptionally beneficial to yourself and others?

For example, your greatest gift is the ability to listen. You are a tremendous encourager and uplifter. You have a gentleness about you.

And you have a tremendous gift of discernment: you do not go out hither and yon telling everybody in your life all that you are thinking and feeling.

Take a look at the lies that you have been holding on to. Challenge them: is this the truth? Look at the weaknesses that you think you have and find ways to remove the 'judgments' that you have around those qualities.

Take pleasure in the simple things, like drinking water. Take the glass of water, sit it in the sunlight, let the rays from the sun shine upon it, bless it in your hands, and then drink it.

And know this well. Understand this clearly. You *must* understand this clearly. You are whole. Complete. You were created that way. You are, each of you, a beloved child of God.

It is only your mind that sees it differently.

The blockages that you are still holding on to—do not fear—they are crumbling one at a time.

So be at peace.

Keep your mind on that which is good, kind, noble, and trust worthy[33]. Meditate on these words, with ease. Live and breathe and soak up their light.

Indeed, it is good to spend time quietly, and call in that peace, as you are known to do.

Be still and know the great meditation words: that his peace was given to you and it is available at any time[34].

He left you peace, but you have to access it.

A Prison of our Own Making

We are dis-eased with how far we walk away from who we are

A year or two prior to all of this, just after finishing my graduate degree, I completed a Huna Healing certification.

In the course, we meditated with the intention of reconnecting with our inner child. The first step was to think of a joyful place that you can bring yourself to.

For me, my memory was of being in the water on the southwest side of Maui, Hawaii (Wailea beach). I closed my eyes and brought myself back to a family trip that we had taken just a couple of years before. My two little girls were elated to be in the water with me, jumping the waves, while their father watched our bags, willingly sitting under a shaded tree, reading a book in peace.

For context, this family trip was also a congratulatory trip for me. For us all actually, since it was happening just after I completed my master's degree; the time it took me to complete the degree was stressful and challenging on the entire family. So, what better way to celebrate than checking something off our bucket list! And the air points I had accumulated over four years were going to get us all there!

So there we were, in full congratulatory mode, thigh-deep in the water, with our backs to the tide and our heads cranked back to see what type of wave was forming behind us. The waves were unpredictable at best: a small wave could knock us off our feet and a big wave, that we were prepared to take us to the seashore, would sometimes produce an underwhelming tousle. But it always produced laughter. We spent hours in that water but it didn't take me long to realize that there was no rhyme or reason to this. I was at the beautiful mercy of this gravitational wonder. I had absolutely no control, and I embraced it.

That realization was one of my favourite memories of the trip, coupled with the laughter, and the joyful locked-eye looks between me and my darling girls. I saw through to the window of their souls on that beach. We were just there, simply present in the moment, where nothing else mattered. At one point, I thought to call out to my husband to take a picture. But, the sounds of the waves, the laughter, the smiles, and that indescribable feeling of connection—both to them and to everyone and everything—were burned into my memory.

And that would have to do.

So, yes, this was a beautiful memory that I could easily bring myself back to for the meditation. My heart even started pumping a little harder as I visualized myself there. Back to the jumping, back to the ridiculous child-like chuckling that makes you feel like you have a lump in the back of your throat and brings tears to your eyes if you think about it for too long. Back to looking over at my little girls, and taking in their happiness, their joy, the adventure of it all.

Then, I looked over my other shoulder and there she was: this little girl with ringlet-curls. In the midst of our laughter, she was just standing there with slumped shoulders looking down. No smiles. No jumping. No laughter. She was *so* sad that she captured my attention. And then she looked up at me and I realized that this little girl was me.

This sad little girl was *me.*

And without a word spoken, her eyes told me the reason that she was sad and confused: why was I giving so much love to the girls on my right that I had forgotten about her?

Even as I write this now, the tears flow.

It is so easy to do this. We sink ourselves into the identity of who we *think* we are. We take on roles and we give everything we have to others. There is little left for ourselves.

And then we wonder why we start to feel angry, or tired, or why we get sick. We are dis-eased with how far we walk away from who we are. We continue to go down a path of our own making—a prison of our own making—trying to cope in the only way we know how: listening to our inner dialogue that often gives us bad advice.

And it happens. All. The. Time.

So after that painful revelation, I started working on my own self-care. And it was hard. It is often very hard to pull away from all the obligations: 'Well, I'm certainly not going to miss their birthday,' or 'There are dishes to be done,' or 'I have this project due,' or 'I'll just do this one last thing and then maybe get to my stuff...'

Shall I go on?

So, I started making more time for me: I went rollerblading *with* myself—note the distinction: I went *with myself* not *by myself.* I went to a vegan restaurant I had wanted to go back to. I bought myself a pretty scarf. I started doing guided meditations more frequently to try to reconnect.

During the first few meditations, I had a hard time visualizing what I looked like as a child, so I found a cute picture of me when I was four or five years old that my Mom had framed for me. I put it in my bathroom to try to resurrect the memories.

Then, a little while later—probably months into the process—I was in the middle of a meditation that had calmly led me in to a peaceful grassy field. A new image of me popped into mind. I felt so excited that that memory had resurfaced that it brought a smile to my face.

This cute little curly girl, this little TL, started coming toward me and I just stood there watching. She walked right up to me, looked me in the eyes, and smacked me in the face. It was the slap of a toddler—so relatively gentle—but it still stung.

I figured this meant I had a little more work to do.

So, for almost two years, I worked on being kinder and gentler to myself. I worked on my language, and tone. So, 'Come on TL! This isn't rocket science! You've got a deadline' became 'It's ok, TL. This isn't rocket science. You've got this.'

The words are so similar, but oh so very different.

Considering all that was on my plate, I was pretty committed to this. And, I thought I was doing a pretty stellar job of finding little pockets of time in my day (i.e. I could take 10 minutes out of my lunch and do a relatively effective meditation with my headphones on). But I found that it just took the edge off. I was only making minimal progress.

And then the job went away.

So in between the journal reviewing, and the purging, and the inspiration board creating, I decided that it was also time to dust off my to-do list and start getting some of them done.

One item popped off the page more than the others: 'pics of me—every year'.

So I borrowed a couple of boxes of my parents' photo albums and started the task of sifting through page after page. I took pictures of the pictures with my phone. Through this process, I saw pictures of me that I had never seen before. I found many that I had forgotten about. I finally got copies of some of my favourites that I didn't have a copy of. And all of the pictures stirred up my memory bank enough to lock in some of those lost and hidden memories. They made me smile. I scrolled through them many, many times. I showed them to my girls. I showed them to my husband. He laughed a lot. He also smiled a lot.

All of these things that I felt urged to do were repeatedly reminding me of what I had forgotten.

Prompting me of what I needed to remember.

And then, in that same grassy field, that cute little curly girl walked toward me again. That same little TL stood right in front of me. She looked up at me again.

And she reached up her arms and gave me a hug.

I was making progress.

And over time, the hug turned into us holding hands and walking through that grassy field together, arms swinging back and forth.

And then, so beautifully, one day, in that grassy meadow we met up with the source. And we just walked along looking at the sun-filled sky, filled with an indescribable feeling of peace that no one understands, like it was an every day thing.

And shouldn't it be?

It was goose bump inducing. It felt just right. I was home.

Broken Heart

It is not easy to do soul-searching

Recently, I met up with an old work colleague, and he quite innocently asked me what I'd been up to. I had asked myself this question in my own mind too. And in response to my own question, I would often have to fight the urge to justify how I had been spending my time.

Even as I spoke aloud my response to my friend's question, I was curious to hear my own answers: the things I focused on were laced, albeit mildly, with words of validation. It was as if I needed to justify, even to myself, that I hadn't been bored, or something like that. I found it equally interesting to hear what I omitted from my summary.

I said something like this: 'Well, I spent the early part of the fall negotiating my package and sorting out finances. Then I purged my house. Then, for the month of November, I headed out west to visit some family and friends. Then it was Christmas. In January, I started an intense yoga instructor certification, which brought me to the Grand Canyon for my one-week final retreat in early May. And soon, I'm heading out east on a road trip with the girls for the month of July. Then I'll figure out my next steps. I've decided to take an intentional one-year 'sabbatical', at least.'

In ways, this was an acceptable answer. It was an honest question, but one that wasn't really begging for a detailed play by play. His response was kind, and compassionate. But it got me to thinking...

My answer kind of made me look like an entitled brat.

Or maybe I was a little perturbed that I didn't tell him the root of the story, the *truth* in the story. Yes, perhaps I was annoyed that I didn't talk about the core elements that made up the beauty of this time off, the pieces of the story that bring me to tears of gratitude almost daily. *That* was the missing piece.

And in all fairness, some people you simply can't share that level of information with as easily.

I recently had someone ask me what my typical day looks like. When I told her, she said, "that all sounds like filler."

So yes, some people wouldn't understand.

But they don't need to.

And, there is a difference between filling your day, and feeling fulfilled.

Either way, I share it with you now.

All of what I said was honest. But what I had left out was the soul-searching element of the yoga certification. I didn't mention that I had signed up for the course thinking that I was knocking an item off on my bucket list, but, in fact, the course knocked *me* off my feet by giving me the chance to do some deep self-questioning. It was exactly what I needed, even though I didn't know it at the time.

Call it what you want, but I knew after the first class that I was exactly where I needed to be—and I was lucky enough to be there for five months straight.

I had many moments when I just shook my head and laughed: here I was thinking all this time that I had collected all of the 'reasonable data' to confirm that a yoga certification made sense, but the man upstairs had other plans. And those plans are always better than anything my imagination could conjure up.
I will be grateful for that opportunity for the rest of my life.
I tried my best to summarize the experience a few days after:

"Last week, I experienced an earth-shattering, heart-wrecking, purely transformative week.
I'm still processing.
It is not easy to do soul-searching.
Rooted in the mountains of Arizona, I picked up untruths that I've held on to for 10, 20, 30+ years, broke down the myocardium-like layers surrounding my heart, and dissolved them.
They were left on the mountain.
They no longer hold a place here in my tender heart.
My body, mind, soul, and strength were challenged to the extreme. The weather outside that turned from rain, to sleet, to sun mirrored the changes happening inside.
Shouts of encouragement overpowered the doubts in my head. Even my glutes gave up and asked for help.
There is power in release. It makes space for the beautiful unexpected.
May we all reach for such things..."

Because whatever it is that we hold on to, it layers itself around our heart. It becomes a protective barrier to keep us from getting hurt. And experience after experience, layer after layer, our heart is left surrounded and shielded from harm.

And it is counterintuitive to release something we, ourselves, put in place to protect us.

Just breathe.

Just let it go...

I didn't explain that I had pushed myself too far, and I desperately needed a break.

I didn't say that the best way I knew how to show leadership in this world is to highlight the importance of taking a pause in your life; slowing down and embracing the 'anti-busy' side of things; taking time to recover rather than running back to work from your Nanny's funeral, or from the hospital after heart surgery.

I didn't let on that I had to stop the constant striving and that I needed desperately to reacquaint with myself; I had to recalibrate what I was doing all of this for. I also didn't mention that I wanted to have some time with my two darling girls who were growing up far too fast. I didn't explain that my pursuit of success—if we can call it that—might have emasculated my husband (more on this later).

All the things I never said...

That my old way of decision-making was primarily based on fact and data, calculated next steps, and reasonable analytics, but now I had the freedom to just be in the flow. For the first time in as long as I can remember, I was able to follow flash-of-light thoughts in my mind that I felt called to do in the moment. I had the freedom and the time to listen to the thoughts and ideas that came to me that felt just right. And many of the things that came to mind were hopes and dreams buried in the midst of my every day task list, and my adult-learned logical mind, that I hadn't had room to even think about, until now.

That I now had the time to be the friend and person I always hoped to be, rather than being too busy to be truly present with those I love.

That I had started noticing that the depth of discussions I was having with my circle of friends and family members just seemed to change. People were telling me things that I never knew about them. People felt more comfortable being vulnerable around me. I don't think they changed, but rather they were responding to a change in me.

That I always felt on the perimeter of things, or on a bridge between two things. I always felt that people from either side could come on to the bridge, or I could walk over to either side of the bridge and there would be a nice connection. But it never felt where I belonged. Ultimately, they would go back to their side and I would remain on the bridge, and this saddened me. But I'm realizing that I *am* the bridge.

I am the bridge.

And this is a glorious thing. It provides a solid foundation in the storm. It keeps you safe from harm. It lets you calmly and safely come to the water. It's like a helping hand to cross over to the unknown.

And finally, most sadly, I didn't explain that I was able to spend an unforgettable amount of time with a dear aunt who was in the advanced stages of COPD (chronic obstructive pulmonary disorder). Our time was so precious to me, even the rougher days.

One day I had to gently push her to let me come visit her, as she was feeling miserable and clearly stated that she wanted to be alone. It wasn't like me to push. I wanted to respect her and allow her some semblance of control in a world she was living where she had no control. Then she said, "You know what, never mind. Just come if you want to come, no one else listens to what I have to say, so why should you?"

That dear sweet soul was hurting.

I told her that I most certainly wouldn't come if she wasn't feeling up for company. But I also told her what was stuck in my mind's eye: I had all the ingredients to bring over to make her onion cheese pie recipe and I had sewn a little bag for her that would hold her remote control for her bed. And her response was, "Oh, please come. You're so good for my soul." So, I went.

And that was our last time together in her old school house home.

Trust your gut—that still small voice—that voice in the stillness. Take time to listen to it. Action it, and don't delay.

But you need space in your life to hear such things.

And you need a 'broken heart' to welcome in such things.

And interestingly, as I write this, Ed Sheeran's lovely song "Autumn Leaves"[35] comes on my playlist like it was waiting for me to finish writing that last sentence.

The music comes in as if my whole life has a soundtrack.

Parts of this song were quoted in the eulogy I delivered when she passed away, which prompted me to remember another moment with her that I will treasure forever. A moment that I never would have had if I had rushed back to work:

I was sitting with my aunt on her couch. We were holding hands in silence. After a little while, she looked up at me and said, "This is all I need," and squeezed my hand.

I merely offered my hand and a solid ground of love while she swirled through her life storm.

Isn't that all that any of us really ever need?

Hide and Seek

Smothering the thoughts I needed to get out

So, clear as day, like the trip out west, and the yoga instructor training, I felt that it was now time to focus more on my writing. The 'why' behind it wasn't clear, but I tried not to put myself in a corner by narrowly defining the outcome of what I was doing. I did catch myself saying that I think I'm writing a book. But I also found myself adding that I'm trying not to restrict it to one thing or another, and that what I know for sure is that, for now, it's what *I* need to hear.

And this is opposite of what we learn: we are told to set detailed goals and follow a defined path to get there. But the 'magic' happens when we follow our heart and do something because our intuition tells us that it's needed, even if you can't make sense of it.

A still small voice tells us that it is so.

And so, I write.

The writing is for me. And, perhaps as I creep closer to the age of 50, it is also a 'reference guide' for my girls when they draw closer to adulthood.

When I read what I have written, I get tingly all over, as if something that I had forgotten is integrating its way back inside me.

The mere act of writing is the goal.

That is all.

It's similar with next steps after the yoga instructor certification. The logical question is whether I will open up a yoga studio. Fair enough. But how do I confidently say that I feel that the yoga will fit in to something bigger, but I don't know exactly what that is yet? It just sounds a little weak.

But I say it anyway, and accept the outward vulnerability of it all because it's truth.

And this will age me when I say that it reminds me of an entry I wrote in my first diary—over three decades ago—that said, "Everyone thinks that I'm going to be a teacher, but I think I'm going to do something bigger than that." This is no insult to teachers in the school system, but I knew, even at the ripe age of 13 that my purpose was in a teaching capacity, but not a teacher in the traditional sense of the word: my purpose was something less defined. And I was ok with that. I was ok with not having a full-fledged, black-and-white, clearly stated goal.

And it sometimes makes the story more interesting.

So on a quasi-daily basis, after the girls are on their school bus, I do my morning reading, prayer, meditation, and yoga. Then, I get to the point where I just *need* to write. I just know in my heart that I need to get something down 'on paper'.

And sometimes it is only one sentence that comes during the meditation, and I type it out, and nothing else comes: that is all for that day. And other times, an expression comes to mind that I have already written like, 'depths of my diaphragm'. So that day's task is to look that up in my writing, and to hear, to see, to re-read, and to absorb something that I already wrote.

Those days, I simply need to hear the guidance again.

And it is as though all of the things I'm writing have been sitting in my mind for ages, patiently waiting for their turn to come out and play. These things may have been content to be 'stuck' in the back of my mind, buried at the bottom of a pile of junk, trivialities, traumas, and whatever you want to call the things that we hold on to that we know we should really let go of.

But now, they were tired of waiting. They were tired of this game of hide and seek.

And the release that happened in Arizona got them further ahead in the line, so to speak, so now they were happy.

And that, I fully believe, was the real reason for my time off. None of what I had done this year ended up being what I thought it was—it was all so much deeper than that. It was greater than anything that I could have imagined: it was intimate, it was a chance to let go, it was an opportunity to detach from the things that I was holding on to. It was a chance to do some inner purging and get rid of the stuff that was smothering the thoughts I needed to get out.

All it needed was for me to take the risk, to have faith, to let go of the need to understand the 'why' behind it all, to listen and to follow what my gut was telling me to do, even if it made no sense at all.

That was 'all'.

And man alive, it wasn't always easy. For any spouses out there reading this, perhaps you're taking pity on my poor husband.

Now, I'm a pretty good communicator, which likely helped Gareth to try to wrap his head around my 180°, since it was not like me to just stop. But in the end, this was me doing what I knew I needed to do.

In my mind, I was relatively calm, because there was a peaceful knowing. But oh, how much harder it is to explain such a thing.

And the writing didn't really start happening until the late spring. I had asked myself a few times through the fall, winter, and early spring why I wasn't writing. The thought crossed my mind whether it was because I was afraid of failure. Just in case, I tried to keep my biggest creative block—cleaning—in check because I knew I could easily use it as a distraction. But in the end, I didn't think it was any of that; I felt in my heart that the time would come soon to do such things.

And that time was now.

Indeed, the thoughts were flowing through me feverishly, now that I let go of looking for a way to define it.

The brief guidance I heard during this time was:

The time will come. What is the rush?

For now, it will not be perfect.

Right now, it will not make sense, but that is ok. Who says what is *perfect* anyway? Start with small steps.

You are not writing this book...

This book is writing you.

Wireless Connection

There is a reconnecting of the bulbs

So some people ask me, "How do you know when something feels right?"

Sometimes, I know because the thought gives me 'truth bumps[36]'.

Or, the knowing may fill my eyes with tears—as if I had just remembered something that I had forgotten that was so incredibly important—as if I had just discovered something that I was desperate to find—as if I had just uncovered something that I had longed to know all of my life, without even knowing that it was missing.

All at the same time.

And as I've tried my best to explain, it's as though my fingers and my brain are firing without my knowing what is going on. I'm playing catch up to what is happening before my eyes.

And it's ok to let the universe take over.

It's divinity alive and well.

I am a vessel. You are a vessel too.

Be the vessel. Just let it be.

Let it happen.

It's like a wireless connection.

Because when it does happen, it's pure joy. When you are flowing, you wonder why you spent so much time doing all the other stuff that occupied your time.

For me, I am flowing when I write.

And I just know it's what I'm meant to do.

But, sometimes it's a small thing that you 'just know': someone just pops in to your mind and you think 'I should call them'. So you do it: you call them out of nowhere, and they *really, really* needed that call.

That's listening to the still small voice.

That's training your mind how to listen.

Sometimes it's bigger things. I remember working at a job a good while back and I was commuting 2 hours each way and on the way to work one day I prayed for a sign whether I should quit. I walked into my boss' office for our 9 a.m. meeting and she said that she didn't know how I was doing it, that she lived just around the corner and was having a hard time keeping up.

I took that as an obvious sign.

I walked back into my office and picked up the phone. But I had to ask myself what number I was dialing. My Dad picked up, as I was asking myself why I had called him. I asked him for the name of his travel agent and had to ask myself why I was asking for this.

In this case, I wasn't consciously aware of what I 'knew'; I was trying to catch up to what was happening.

Then I called the travel agency, not knowing why and booked the last seat on a flight to see my Nanny.

And *this* was exactly what I needed. It was exactly where I knew—albeit only subconsciously—that I needed to be.

God had heart-shaped that place on a map for me.

So, I was not unfamiliar with such a thing.

And then, just recently, I saw a friend at a gathering, but we didn't get much time to chat. So, I sent him a note and said, "I'm not sure why, and don't take this the wrong way, but I can't get you out of my mind ☺. I feel like I need to meet with you." And his response was equally fun. He wrote back and said, "I know. I was hoping to get more time to connect with you too. Not sure why but yes. Let's."

He had something to tell me.

So we met. Another friend I had been trying to connect with was there as well. And after a great discussion, these lovely old friends laid their hands on me.

And this is what they heard:

You are tender and gentle-hearted.

It is worth noting that hearing this alone was a tearjerker. I have a little rock with the words 'be known for your gentleness[37]' written on it. I see the rock daily as it holds my bathroom door open. But I had told a friend last year that I might have to give up on that one.

Perhaps not.

They also told me:

There is an emptying of your bag happening.

This emptying out is just a gentle God helping you to connect all of the things he's given you to his 'life power heart'. You are like a lamppost providing people with light and direction. And it's like the lamppost is being wired and connected. Or, like Christmas lights: there is a reconnecting of the bulbs that weren't working and suddenly they all spring to life.

It's like God is holding your timeline and breathing on it, making things come to life, even things you'd forgotten you'd prayed for. He is dusting off his past words to you, giving you back things he always meant for you to have, and he's breathing life into your life.

As you are creating the space for him to bring things to life, he's going to bless your words, your voice, and your presence for many. That's exciting.

Indeed.

And during the discussion, we talked about having a 'dialogue with God' in instances where you want to understand what direction you should go, what to do in a certain situation, or whether something is truth.

Because, you don't always have the advantage of knowing: 'Script' it out.

We did this when we met and the dialogue looked something like this:

Do you think I'm intelligent?

🦋 You are connected to me.

Own the truths that God speaks to you when you surrender something to him.

My friend sent me a follow up after we met and said that he found himself saying to someone how many gifts God has given me. He was able to use me as an example of how someone so bright—in mind and heart—could believe a lie that they weren't smart.

It really helped them.

And that really helped me too.

The Dialogue

Just breathe

What would you have me do?

🦋 Keep doing what you are doing.

I'm anxious.

🦋 Love your feelings.

I'm in unchartered ground.

🦋 You asked for rest. I have given you everything you have ever asked for.

I'm not sure what I want now—but I want to be sure that my will is aligned with yours. Can you give me clarity on my purpose?

🦋 Little Larry, your dear friends Melanie and Diana, your Mom, Gareth, your girls, you, your Aunt Heather, your friend Sharon, your Aunt Marly.

But how can I make money doing what I love / what my purpose is?

🦋 It will come.

I don't like that answer.☺

🦋 Don't be so cerebral about it. Just keep writing.

Thank you for the releasing that has happened, especially in Arizona. I really am enjoying being off, and having some down time, but I'm not wanting to lose something along the way that you don't want me to lose.

🦋 I won't let you forget.

I'm having such a hard time with Gareth and feeling like he's hard to be around.

🦋 He's a mirror.

I feel like I'm just giving myself some of these answers. How can I tell that I'm having the dialogue with you?

🦋 I am the peace that no one understands[38]. Is your heart opening?

Am I doing right by you?

🦋 You need to be calmer with the girls.

So what would you have me do?

🦋 Drink more water. Just breathe. Bring out their light. Give yourself time to *be*.

Total Recall

We lock it in our vault of memories

A few years ago, in the fray of full-time graduate school and working full time, I created a new list called 'things to do when I finish my master's. One of the things written on the list was to have a grade 8 reunion.

Again, I really didn't know *why*, but I knew I *really* wanted to do this.

Either way, after sitting on this for two years after finishing the degree, I came across it in the middle of the summer—about a month before my job ended—and I thought, 'I'm just going to send a little message to the classmates I'm already connected with—as informal as it is—because if I don't, I might never get to it.' And that request for a small informal get together quickly turned into the real deal.

When I told my youngest sister that I had put together a steering committee, of sorts, to pull the reunion together, her response was, "of course you are." Then she said something like "kill me now" about the thought of attending such a reunion for herself.

Fair enough.

Actually, many other people asked me why I thought to do this. The quick, and likely easiest, answer is, 'I have no idea.' And this is true. I really didn't. As I thought about it a little more, it even confused me. The fact that I was leading this reunion was a little odd: I had moved in the summer after grade 7, so I was in a brand-new school for my grade 8 year. Many of the people that would be attending the reunion were in my life for only that year. So, why pull together this group? What was the motivation?

After rooting through some old things in my memory box (a little more closely) it began to make more sense: grade 8 was a defining year for me.

One shining memory from that year was attending a beautiful weeklong retreat that was life changing. It helped me embrace the quirks that made me *me*. It gave me more confidence. It was another way of staying in touch with my 'mini TL'.

My other motivation was that my grade 8 teacher, 'Mr. D' (or Carl as I now *try* to call him) was my favourite teacher and was part of a milestone point of my life.

So much so, that I reached out to him before the reunion and we decided to meet up for coffee.

And after catching up on over 30 years of life, I thanked him for being the best teacher I ever had.

With tears in both of our eyes, he said that he was so glad to hear that because he had always wondered whether I had felt that he had betrayed me in grade 8.

You see, I had come in to school one day and told him a secret.

And he had no choice but to report it. So now, over 30 years later, I sat in front of him as he told me that he always worried that I thought he had betrayed me. I told him that I had understood that it was his obligation. We cried a few more tears.

There was some releasing and some learning that day: he released that little nagging thought that was stuck in the back of his mind for decades. For me, I was so glad that I listened to that little nudge to connect with him before the reunion. There is nothing better than looking into someone's eyes and feeling a connection, where no words are needed to say what your eyes—the windows to your soul—are telling them.

And what this really taught me is that our memories often fail us.

Sometimes we are so sure of something that happened, that we lock it in our vault of memories and it becomes part of who we are. We allow the illusion to define us.

Our memories simply fail us.

It's like our 'total recall' function has a glitch.

I remembered that the secret was just between the two of us and that I had shared it with some help from above, and maybe a little nudge or two. I didn't recall telling another soul.

But, his story was different. It seems that a couple of friends came with me to speak with him—they were a big part of helping me muster up the courage to tell the truth.

While this may seem like a small part of the story, this was huge for me because I tend to think that I am fiercely independent, and I struggle, at times, to lean on others for support.

I've told myself this do-it-on-your-own story on countless occasions.

Indeed, our memories aren't always dependable. Sometimes, we just *want* to remember things a different way. Sometimes the truth is too painful to bear. Other times, we are just mistaken.

Either way, use extreme caution with them.

So fast-forward to the day of the actual reunion, and it was blissful. While the details may fade over time, here were the highlights as they were still freshly baking in my mind:

I remember one person coming in and giving hugs to everyone she saw, with tears in her eyes.

That alone made it worth the effort.

I remember grins turning into ear-to-ear smiles as people recognized each other, even if it took a second or two.

That also made it worth it.

I remember putting the palms of my hands on the cheeks of an old friend and just soaking up their essence. I felt 13 years old again.

Seeing him, and feeling that 13-year-old me, made it all worthwhile (especially because I think he came as a special favour to me).

But, hands down, my key memory of the evening, that captured my heart, is in this summary I wrote the day after:

> Feeling nostalgic today as I think back to the grade 8 reunion that happened last night. Twenty of us gathered together after over 30 years. It was delightful, incredible, and goose bump inducing. It felt just right.
>
> So I sat back today to think about why...
>
> Some people came because of sheer excitement to reacquaint with people they had lost touch with. Some came out of mere curiosity. Some other people came in the hopes of soaking up some of the contagious-like joy that was building in the weeks leading up to the reunion. And a few people came because of a gentle nudge that came in different forms but served as a reminder that they are loved.

So I walked through the crowd last night, taking it all in with cheerful pleasure, and left with a clear reminder of our interconnectedness. Despite our differences, we really are all the same.

We all yearn to love and to be loved...

...And when you give a tiny, seemingly insignificant, piece of your heart away, it has an impact. Sometimes in ways that you don't hear about for 30+ years. But that little piece of your heart you gave away is returned to you tenfold—if you let it in.

Yes, if you let it in...

Food for Your Soul

Give them wiggle room to grow

A nd some days you just need to cry.
     Maybe you had a bad sleep and woke up on the wrong
side of the bed. Maybe someone said something to you the
night before that is stuck in your head. Maybe it takes you a
little while before you find a reason—a justification—for the
upset. Maybe, despite the striving to figure it out, you still don't
know what's going on in that head of yours and you rack your
brain trying to make some sense of it. You are desperate to
attach the feeling to *something*.

And what you definitely know is that your eyes are filling
with tears, and right now, everything that has been bad in your
life, and everything bad in the world, all seem to be rising up
inside of you and making it worse.

'I can't believe he said that...And I can't believe that bill
was so much higher than expected...And now I have so many
things on my plate, which was what I was trying to avoid...And
maybe I've been doing all of this for nothing...And how am I
going to get through next week...And I can't believe I said that
last week...And what am I going to do when I 'grow up'? And
next week is going to be a gong show...And what the heck am

I complaining about? Stop your whining: there are so many people that have it worse than you...'

Should I go on?

In these times, we would take on the weight of the world's problems on to our own shoulders if we could.

We either need an explanation or an avoidance tactic; we may try to find the root of the issue or we may look for a solution to all of the hypotheticals that bounce around in our minds. Or, we may find a way to sidetrack ourselves.

Either way, let me tell you a secret...

We make the upset an idol.

In other words, we make the 'figuring it out' almost like a thing of worship.

If we can't figure it out, or can't even bear to *try* to understand it, we make distraction the apple of our affection.

Let me tell you that my house can end up looking pretty spotless in times like these.

And through this, our minds are reminded of the stories we've told ourselves for much of our lives. You tell yourself lies like, 'See? You're a fool to be listening to your gut.' You second-guess yourself. You tell yourself that maybe the mockers are right.

And should some small kindness come to you, in this fragile state, it either breaks you down—because you are feeling so undeserving of the kindness that it makes you feel worse—or you have such selective attention, you might not even notice the kindness that has come your way.

Take a deep breath.

Stop analyzing. Stop looking for a reason. Stop trying to find the why behind the why. Stop judging yourself for having the audacity to have a bad day. Stop isolating yourself from the people who would give you love.

Including yourself.

Turn your pre-programmed thinking on its head.

Do nothing but love it. You have a tender heart and it's hurting today. And that's ok.

This too shall pass.

It really will.

And right now, you just need to give yourself a little love. Shower yourself with it. Take a deep breath and let it be.

Know that it all belongs, that everything is sacred, that we all feel that we are lacking wholeness and we are searching for it. We are mad at each other because of what we feel we don't have.

My dear sweet soul—don't be so hard on yourself.

A quick story:

My youngest daughter came home from a recital last night and took out the plant powder packet that was included in the bouquet of flowers she had received from her Nana and Grandpa. She read the instructions.

She then proceeded to get out the measuring cup and add the correct amounts of plant food and water. She left it on the countertop.

The next morning, I came downstairs and noticed that she hadn't put the plant water in the vase with her flowers, so I did it for her.

A little later on, when she was putting her cereal bowl on the counter (that lovely girl cleaning up after herself!), she noticed the empty measuring cup. She immediately started crying crocodile tears and both angrily and devastatingly asked me if I had thrown out her plant water. I looked at her in surprise, as I wasn't too sure why she was so upset. "No, no, my dear girl. I didn't throw it out, I put it in your vase so it would feed your plants."

"But I didn't want it with the other flowers! I wanted it to be a flower on its own!" Her voice was raised, and tears were still streaming down her face.

I looked at the anger and sadness on her face, and then looked at the powder packet.

And then I understood.

So I said softly, "Oh honey, the powder packet isn't powder to grow a new flower, it's food for your flowers in the vase. So, I fed your flowers for you."

And I walked over and gave her a big hug. "Oh, you sweet girl."

"I'm sorry. I thought the powder was to grow a new flower," she replied as she hugged me back.

"That's ok. You didn't know and now you do. Oh, my dear, sweet girl, everything's fine." And the hug continued for a little longer.

So why does this story come to mind?

Because we are so much kinder and gentler to these little ones than we are to ourselves.

We love them. We speak softly. We have more patience with them. We hug them. We laugh with them. We encourage them. We spend time with them. We give them wiggle room to grow. We tell them that it's ok.

We are often in a higher vibration with them.

But, in the next breath, our own inner dialogue can turn harsh. We blame ourselves for things. We hold on to guilt for things we've done. We tell ourselves to push through it, to have another coffee, to not be so foolish. We shave a little time off of our sleep routine to fit another thing or two into our day. And those little things add up.

And then we get mad at ourselves when the accumulation of little stresses catch up with us and we have an off day.

Yes, alas, we are often in a lower vibration with ourselves.

I'll say it again: my dear sweet soul, don't be so hard on yourself.

'Come into the water.' It's fine in here.

Treat yourself like you would that little child. Give yourself some wiggle room. Don't strive for perfection.

When you feel like you've messed up just say, 'That's ok. You didn't know, and now you do,' and that's the end of that.

Shower yourself with the love you save for everyone else.

It is food for your soul.

And then entered some extra guidance:

The peace must be found within. The peace must be steady, with the certainty that all is well. It is not a competition or a race. Just take it step by step.

Speak truths in the face of the storm. If you can do this, it is an indication that you are able to go into the water, and stand with the waves crashing by you—when some of them will crash you down—and even if you fall face down, you come up with the laughter. There is never any danger here.

And for many, there has always been the danger. There has never been the convincing that things work out for them.

When each one of you is in the midst of the wounding, you are all like a small child. This is when you need tenderness to come in. Don't try to remove it. Sit and hold yourself in with source energy.

Allow yourself to be angry, to have those feelings of tremendous hopelessness and failure. Let it be. It has nothing to do with who you are.

It is just window dressing that you put upon yourselves.

But when the darkness comes you seem to feel that that is all you are; that you are dark and there is not a bit of light in you.

In these times, it is important to sit in moments of quiet meditation. Remove the demands of the world and detach from any thoughts, opinions, and ideas.

All is allowed to just be as it is: there is nothing to do; there is nothing to prove; there is nothing to ask...

It is letting go of all the ways of the world. It is returning back to that place from even before the forming of your being in the earthly realm. It is returning to that state of positive love.

And when each of you are in this place of darkness, you do tend to go to the place when you feel that you do not have a friend in the world. You have a hard-enough time dealing with it yourself to think about having those around you feel the discomfort of seeing you in the dark. But, you must show yourself some compassion and call them forward.

You have just forgotten who you are.

And when there is too much airplay of this shadow aspect of one's self, one of the best things to do for yourself is to go and have a nap—shut it down for a while. Lie yourself down on your pillow with the words 'all is well' and remind yourself of how grateful you are to have the comfort of the pillow and your fresh sheets and the warm blanket.

ALL is well.

All IS well.

Heavy Loads

Some things aren't meant to sit around for too long

If you think this whole process was seamless with my husband coming home, kissing me on the cheek, and super happy to hear about my day, you're quite mistaken. In fact, the words, unsupportive, saboteur, jealous, frustrated, and anxious all come to mind. He questioned me. He was skeptical. At times, there were mild tones of mockery.

And then there were times when he seemed quite supportive—although I could never tell if he was just going through the motions *trying* his best to understand.

At least he was trying.

And this is fair: it was difficult to understand from the outside. People saw me putting my heart and soul in to the type of work I did. For 17 years, I was filled with a passionate fire that seemed inextinguishable.

But every chapter has an ending.

And what many people didn't know was that there were many fires burning in my heart. The only difference was one was taking over a bigger space than the others. It was talked about more than the others. It was paying the bills.

And then the big bill (our mortgage) went away and everything seemed to click into place. Like one small turn of a kaleidoscope can completely change what you see, I was now looking at things differently. This was a gift. This was an opportunity to revisit the things stuck so long in the back of my mind that they seemed almost lost and forgotten. Some I had completely forgotten about. So many of the things throughout the year helped me to remember, and stillness or lack of busyness was one of them.

It may seem like that was a tiny thing to happen to have such a drastic effect. I even had someone highlight to me that they thought I could have higher hopes and desires than paying off a mortgage. True enough, but for me, it was freedom personified. I'm not naïve enough to ignore that my kids may soon want to go to university, or that I love to travel, or that retirement is a real thing. This all costs money.

But I'm also not naïve enough to ignore the back-burner fires that have stayed on minimum heat for too long.

It was time for them to come forward, get fired up, and shine.

And luckily I didn't have to go through much of the messing-with-my-head stage that many people experience when they lose their job. Did the thought cross my mind to take this personally? Yes, absolutely, but it certainly wasn't all consuming. And I think it helped that my gut told me it was coming.

And the attitude you choose is everything.

But, what also helped enormously was a course I had taken in graduate school. It was a gut-wrenching residential week where we went through assessment-after-assessment that left many people in a state of vulnerability and doubt. And then we were given assignments working in teams with people who were unintentionally pushing each other's buttons. One of the hardest tasks of the week was pushing through the insecurities that were boiling up in each of us. *That* messed with my head.

And one thing that the course prompted me to remember was that work wasn't the only thing that defined me. There were many other things on my list—creative in nature—that I could easily shift my attention to.

I had thought of this often over the past year. As I saw it, the *things* on my list weren't necessarily changing, but rather, their *sizes* were shifting: work was now in smaller font and the others were getting bigger.

There was opportunity here.

I would be lying if I said that I was 100% positive, 100% of the time. Every now and then, the pragmatic me—often prompted by a more logical person rubbing off on me—asked a few questions:

But, what will you do for work? You can't possibly let that piece of your life shrivel up? What will people think? I have some projects to work on, but after I finish those, what will I do with my time? Should I be more concerned than I am about this?

However, for the most part, I wasn't concerned about that, because the largest voice in my inner dialogue was telling me it was time to take a rest. I just *knew* it was time. Like when I met my husband-to-be and knew that he was the one. I really just *knew* and there is no way to explain it other than that.

So, I enjoyed the present moment more than I can recall doing—ever in my life. Thinking back, I realized that I had moved out when I was 16 and had been working ever since. There were some small breaks along the way, but they were maternity/parental leaves in my thirties, or due to unexpected events like getting hit by a drunk driver in my early twenties, or needing heart surgery just after I turned 40. In all cases, I returned to work and was back in action quicker than expected.

Now was the time to rest, to enjoy, to be filled up, to laugh, to make better, to heal, to let go, to forgive, and to remember.

And those few questions, that popped their head up from time to time, calmly and respectfully took their place on the back burner where my hopes and dreams had been stored for far too long.

It wasn't time to answer those questions.

And I was ok with that.

What a blessing to not have to schedule things weeks (or months) in advance. What a pleasure to wake up in the morning and (a few small obligations aside) be able to see where the 'wind' would take me that day.

So the joyful question that I had never been able to ask myself before was: what did my heart *want* to do today?

No more gotta, gotta, gotta.

And a lot more wanna, wanna, wanna.

But in the end all the things I thought would be different were the same.

Yes, during all that work time, I had convinced myself that if only I had more time, if only I were at home, if only this, if only that, things would be different. Certainly then, my mind wouldn't be going mile-a-minute trying to figure out how to fix all the things I felt were broken.

And, as a classic defence mechanism, I would do the one thing that would keep those thoughts in check: keep myself *beyond* busy. When I was in graduate school, balancing that full-time load, with full-time work and home responsibilities, I was almost absent-free of doubt, and guilt, and self-judgment. I truly had no time for such things.

But what a way to turn things off! How absurd it sounds now. Yet, how perfectly logical, and admittedly blissful, it was at the time.

If I couldn't make an event, it was a relatively guilt-free, matter-of-fact decision. Many times, I really, honestly, couldn't fit another thing in my day. It forced me to hyper-prioritize so I attended the most essential things, and let the other things pass me, and my emotions, by.

And it could also be that expectations were lowered because people knew I was in the midst of a juggling act and that I was holding my breath half of the time just trying to keep my head above water.

I was in pure survival mode.

During that time, I focused solely on the critical. I made sure no deadlines at work or school were missed. I made sure the kids were fed and had relatively good hygiene. I checked in with the husband from time to time, mostly to be sure that our shared logistical duties were in check.

The problem was that there were lots of things in the middle of these two extremes. Many random thoughts surfaced that had to be set aside (that is what to-do lists are great for!). But there were many other thoughts that tried to surface, even for a split second, that were denied access. Many such thoughts didn't fit on a to-do list, so they were put in a categorical mental 'pile' and left for later.

But there are repercussions to such things. Sometimes the thing you leave for a while just sits and patiently waits (like doing a grade 8 reunion). Other times, they can fester.

Just this morning, I grabbed the overflowing laundry bin from our main bathroom and started sorting it. The stuff on the surface wasn't too bad, but as I got in deeper and pulled out the still-damp dishcloths, the grass-filled socks, and some mud-stained clothes, the smell at the bottom of the bin was offensive. The state of affairs in my laundry room wasn't pretty.

Kind of like the state in my head at that time.

Some things aren't meant to sit around for too long. They need to be attended to.

So then, after graduate school was done, I started playing catch up. I started tending to some of the easier tasks on my to-do list—the clearly black and white ones. The thoughts I had pushed away took a little while to resurface. I think I had been so harsh with some thoughts that had tried to surface, that some were even afraid to rear their tiny little heads.

And I talked myself into believing that a lot of these thoughts would go away if things were different.

Thoughts like, 'My house is never clean', and 'I wish I had more patience with my husband and my kids', and 'Man, if only I had more time, the projects I could finish!' And I blamed all the thoughts, and my behaviours, on external things like having a job, or the weather, or our social/extra-curricular schedules. I used it as a lame excuse to justify my mood.

Yes, things would most certainly be different if I had more time.

My husband often said, with slight disappointment in himself, that he really wished that he could provide enough for the family that I wouldn't have to work.

So we both used it as a scapegoat.

And then—poof—the job went away. And my productivity ran wild! I got a number of things knocked off the project list. I was calmer.

But then I came to some tough revelations.

I realized that I actually wasn't as patient of a person as I thought I would be. I was still flying off the handle at times. In my previous state of fatigue and survival-mode antics, I had unintentionally allowed my girls some wiggle room for extra child-like naughtiness. So, while their non-listening habits hadn't changed, I thought that my patience-level would.

But I still lost my patience more than I would like. And I didn't have anything circumstantial to blame it on.

So, there it was: there was a problem with them listening plus there was a problem with my reaction to it.

And I certainly didn't want to tackle the issue by displaying my impatience.

So, I now had the time to realize that I was part of the problem and had to figure out how to fix it. And, in classic irony, it's taking a little time. It's taking patience.

Anyone who knows me is aware of the fact that the cleanliness of my house is likely a bigger focus for me than the average bear. The embarrassment that was my basement, and the not-clean-to-my-expectations upper two floors, was chalked up to not having adequate time to make it just right.

So after I finished purging the house, I was in dismay. I truly had the false impression that if I had more time, and put everything in its place, that it would stay that way.

Strangely, my family didn't share that same expectation.

I was witness to my house going from spotless to disaster in less than an hour. And if you ever want to see a grumpy Mama bear, just come in and mess up my house just after I've spent an entire day on it and watch what happens.

So, I had a good opportunity to test out new approaches in influence, motivation, and keeping calm.

Grateful to be blessed with this time of rest and reflection, there was no way that I was going to let housecleaning distract me. And I certainly was not going to get the family into a new routine of relying solely on me for such things.

I had bigger and better things to do.

So, slowly but surely, things are being figured out. I'm letting go—a little bit—of my own expectations of what a clean house looks like and we're having discussions as a family on how best to get into a routine where cleaning is less like pulling teeth and more on the sugary-sweet side of the spectrum.

I accepted that I had my moments, sometimes for no reason, and sometimes with very, very good reason. So, now my task is to figure out whether I am prepared to let it ruin a perfectly good day or whether I just need to take a deep breath and get on with it.

I also realized that sometimes there are things you 'want' to do that you just don't get around to doing—they just linger on your list for ages and you start to ask yourself whether you would ever do them, even if you had all the time in the world.

Maybe it's just not the right time. Or maybe, just maybe, it is on the list for the wrong reason.

The fact that you don't get to it can be very telling.

No more gotta, gotta, gotta.

No more heavy loads.

So, all the things I thought would be different were the same. But what *is* changing is that they are becoming better understood. They are slowly being addressed. They aren't being thrown into compartments of busyness and written off as collateral damage of making a living for your family. They aren't landing at the bottom of a laundry bin to fester and become a larger problem down the road.

You owe yourself more than that.

Reconciliation

And I pushed myself through the entire day for this

Forgiveness has been ringing in my ears for months. I've made various attempts to list out, think about, and sometimes reach out to, those I've wronged or those whom I felt had wronged me.

I had been granted the time to do such a thing.

I left some of these memories on the mountains of the Grand Canyon.

I released some of these in conversations that were filled with mutual tears.

I feel like I've let go of so, so much.

I feel like I've forgiven 70 times 7[39].

Like the layers of an onion, I keep asking how deep will this go? How is forgiveness *still* in the forefront of my mind?

And then a new day rises to be, one that I'm perfectly grateful for. And then I go and mess it up by allowing myself to let things get under my skin. I allow myself to get perturbed by the rising temperature in my house. It's holding at 26.5 degrees Celsius (just shy of 80 degrees Fahrenheit) but neither my husband nor I are willing to turn on the air. It's a ridiculous, but unspoken yearly competition to see how long we can go without it.

I beat myself up for drinking much more than I should have the night before. I should know better. But, today, I'm stuck in a vulnerable state as I fight through fatigue and the desire to vomit. Today just happens to also be my husband's birthday, so—at his request—I try to prepare for a party in between naps. I'm grumpy and mad at myself for my own miscalculation the night before.

I broke my own rule to never let anyone top up my wine glass but me.

That said, I'm grateful that I don't have anything more than the party on my plate for the day.

So I trudge on through. I slowly but surely prepare the meal, including a vegan cheesecake with homemade strawberry compote, which is my husband's favourite.

Everything is going relatively well. My oldest gladly set the dining room table, and did so beautifully. My youngest created a handmade placemat for her Daddy, and put the cutest little sign on our side door to welcome our expected guests. The girls both helped in the last hour to do some of the last minute 'polishing'.

But Gareth is almost an hour late, and he rushes in and starts putting things down in every which way and runs for a shower. And then the guests arrive, and the volume of his voice starts rising—and so does everyone else's—and so does mine as I try to talk to one of our friends whose hearing aid isn't doing its job as well as he would like.

And now it's almost 9 p.m., and my girls are getting tired and are really antsy to do dessert. But we're expecting more friends to arrive, and so I continue to contend with the "how many more minutes?" question.

Then, Gareth gets preoccupied by starting up a new electronic device he received for his birthday. He left the room in the middle of gifts and started to play with his new toy. He left by himself. In. The. Middle. Of. The. Party. So when people start asking where he went, I get up and find him. I let him know that people are looking for him. And then, our final guests arrive. And, as one would expect, everyone gets up to hug and chat and catch up on things. Things get even louder. These are all good things. They are signs of a great party. But, the cake is starting to melt in the heat.

"How many *more* minutes, Mama?"

Wow, that's starting to become a really good question.

Gareth then decides to make a handcrafted, cucumber-diced gin and tonic for himself. One guest is so intrigued by it, that he asks for one. So off he goes again to make a fresh one. And then another person asks for one, and he's back in the kitchen.

Meanwhile, my youngest is quite upset now, and the crocodile tears are starting to well up: "How many *more* minutes, Mom? I'm tired."

I'm wondering how many more minutes I could contend with this unnecessary chaos?

I stay in the kitchen where it's a little cooler, but also where the dessert is ready to be candle-lit. I assess the situation: the dessert is a little finicky; after it's made, it's put in the freezer to set. Then, it's meant to be just slightly thawed before serving. I had miscalculated when we would be eating dessert, and I really didn't know if putting it in the refrigerator would do the trick. And the girls are tired and have to get up for school the next morning.

Then I wonder if we should do dessert in the kitchen, so I walk in to the dining room to assess this. People notice that I'm a little flustered. I blame it on the heat.

Some people take it personally and assume that I want them to go—ugh—this is the last thing that I want.

I blame it on the soon-to-be-melting cake—which is truth.

So—to a bouncing back-and-forth Gareth—I say that I think we should do cake. In his defence, he doesn't recall that it's time sensitive, and he's in the midst of his blissful birthday party mingling, so he probably isn't too aware that he barked at me and made me feel two inches tall.

And my guests might all feel like I want them to get the heck out of my house.

And I pushed myself through the entire day for this.

Sigh.

So I get through the rest of the evening and finally lay down on my bed.

My eyes are welled with tears.

I was feeling trapped between my old life—my old ways of behaving—and what I thought my new life was supposed to look like. I wasn't there yet, and I was beating myself up for falling back into old habits—for not being perfect.

And only now do I come to the realization of why forgiveness has been ringing in my ears: I had forgotten to circle it back to me.

Despite all that I had released, all of the work I had done to date, I had neglected my own reconciliation.

Driven to the Bone

You do not get angry when your gas tank is empty. You just fill it up

I picked up the phone to call my aunt, and she was talking to her friend on the phone, the friend who I visited out west. And for some reason, for the first time in her life, my aunt decided to conference me in to her conversation. Then, without thinking—to her friend—I blurted out something like "Listen now. I'm thinking that you should fly to Ontario this summer, and we should go on a road trip out east. What do you think?"

She said, "Yes. I think I will".

And that was that.

Then July arrived and it was time for us to pack up the car and make our way on a month-long trip. And I have to say that once that car started, all of the thoughts about 'reconciliation,' 'heavy loads,' 'food for your soul,' and 'total recall' all went away.

It was a life-changing trip reminding me daily, even minute-by-minute, of how life could be.

Then, on the way back home from that glorious trip, my belly started to get in knots. My cerebral mind started to take over and think about next steps, and ask what integration back into the 'real world' looked like.

Before I left on the trip I had told my husband that I thought the long trip was coming at a good time: we needed a break from each other's energy. We were feeding off of each other, and not in a good way.

I had also reminded him of the 'place of refuge' I hoped to buy: a spot to escape to from time to time.

But then, during that trip, feelings of love, happiness, peace, calm, excitement, and joyful expectation ran through my veins for one month straight.

Now, the juxtaposition of how my home life looked seemed too much to bear.

Don't get me wrong. In one way, I was very excited to get back to the comforts of home and to wrap my arms around my husband. But I was also scared of losing touch with the wonderful energy soaring through me.

So, the return home seemed bittersweet.

Admittedly, it also felt a little unfair: I was comparing a worry-free vacation to the sometimes-mundane, often-chaotic, responsibilities of running a home.

But when you catch a hold of something that you have been seeking, when you remember that feeling that you lost and finally found, you do not want to let it go.

And that trip reminded me of who I am.

Now, the end of the trip marked the end of my 'organized plans': the end of knowing my next step.

The entire year, I had 'followed' a rough framework of planned activities: de-clutter, go out west, do the yoga certification, write, go out east.

And again, I did not know *why* I was doing them. I did not care to know the why. I just knew that I was right where I needed to be.

And the reason for it was bigger and better than I could ever have imagined.

There were higher powers at play.

It was one goose bump inducing experience after another.

I had a spring in my step, an open heart, and a clear mind.

But now, I was heading in to hurry-up-and-wait mode.

And I didn't like it.

My intellectual mind had no concrete 'goal' to look forward to, so a minefield of conflict was brewing.

I had learned so much, but still didn't feel perfectly equipped with the tools, or the armour, to keep myself from falling back into old habits.

So here I stood.

Not knowing where my next footstep would take me.

And then the guidance started flowing:

The purpose of the trip was to connect with your inner child, to balance all areas of your life, to love, and to appreciate how far you've come.

You and your girls did exceptionally well on the trip, because you were all little girls: you met each day with wonder, excitement, and joyful expectation.

Now, after that experience, you want to ensure that you can stay in alignment regardless of the externals. This is more difficult to do when you're in the midst of negativity.

For you cannot breathe easy in a room of smoke, my dear.

Take yourself out into some fresh air. Remove what is contributing to your misalignment. You do this by detaching completely from all thoughts and influences that are not in alignment with God. Empty out your mind of what is irritating you. There is no point in getting upset about the situation and giving it power.

You don't go out into a thunderstorm and get angry at it and tell it to stop. You remove yourself. You seek shelter.

Say things like, 'There is nothing to do. This is not life threatening. Life is good.'

Take the importance of the event away by saying things like, 'In five weeks from now, this will mean nothing.'

Soothe yourself into a source of peace.

And, speaking on a frequent basis with God will help you stay on the straight and narrow.

The next theme is to tell a different story. If something that happened in the past comes to mind, don't repeat the story by making the past event repeat itself. Keep yourself buoyant. Remember the good aspects. Focus on what things feel like, and look like, when all is well.

This puts the choice in your hands. Will you allow life energy to flow through you? When it flows, you are full of health.

The purpose is to align yourself at all costs.

You know when you feel aligned. You feel happy, joyful, and at peace. Speak of the things that will keep you there. For example, when you're in traffic, put a guard on your tongue. It's not a matter of not *feeling* the frustration. Just focus and take care of the situation at hand.

Tell yourself that you are doing very well, and that while this is annoying, you know that what you are complaining about, you yourself could do five minutes later.

Give compassion. Give a blessing. Say a simple prayer. Someone else's reactions should not take your peace away.

This does not mean that you deny what is happening. But, rather than using harsh words, just remind yourself that the person is misaligned. It lightens things up. It takes away the intensity of the situation.

You know what it's like to have a knot in your belly. It is this type of situation—one that is turned unnecessarily intense—that causes the pain.

So honour your humanity and cut yourself some slack. Remove all shame, blame, guilt, and you will find life will embrace you fully.

You are very much focused on bringing light into the world. There is great responsibility to this. You need to be careful to stay in this vibration and take guard.

When you get off track, do not fall into frustration, or sadness, or get upset if your initial reflex is to react. It is just a reminder that you have to make a slight adjustment. Just simply say, 'Thank you for the reminder. I was out of alignment. Now I'm back.' You do not get angry when your gas tank is empty. You just fill it up.

It's as simple as that.

You often speak of finding a place of refuge, a restful place to get away. But know that you can find this in one deep breath. There, you find the sacred space to reflect. Don't believe you need an outside place to do that. You just need to do it inside your heart, and inside your mind.

Your project is your own health and wellbeing. Don't make it about other people.

Trust the wisdom of your own soul.

And, call upon spirit all the time.

Never underestimate the contribution you are making in others' lives.

But there is a tendency for you to want to please others, like you owe them something. When you do this, you give up your own power and your own alignment.

The choices are to benefit *them* instead of all.

So, when you are in a situation, ask yourself, 'is this in the best interest of *all* concerned?'

For it is important to keep yourself out of harm's way. People will come to suck the life out of you. They mean no harm but they see you as a life raft and they will take you down if you are not careful.

And you do not give the car keys to one who does not have a full understanding of the rules of the road and the vehicle.

Remember that you do not need to take the logs of negative energy away, but you also do not have to join them in their misery.

Just remind them of who they are. This will bring them closer to source energy.

Remind yourself that it is not selfish to take this time. Rather, it is selfish to not take the time.

You are here to teach others how to stay in alignment in this world. But, my dear, if you allow yourself to be affected by the things around you, how can you possibly teach others to be calm?

A good example is that you cannot teach another language if you don't know how to speak it fluently. Before you can teach it, you need to know it inside and out. First, it is in a controlled away. Over time, it becomes second nature.

You portray it in your bones, like you are 'driven to the bone', in the opposite sense of the expression.

So, notice the triggers. Then, look at how quickly you can remind yourself to snap out of it.

Unless you get that skill, you simply cannot teach it. You simply cannot remind people of their beauty, and the beauty in front of them, when you are hanging out in the past.

So, do not concern yourself about others. Your stability, and your ability to hold a dominant energy, encourages others to do the same.

It kindles in people what they need to remember.

You are not alone.

You have one provider.

Everything is already in your vortex.

So do not fret, there are lots of great things waiting.

Trainspotting

I'll meet you at the next station if you're there

I wake up in a cold sweat. I hardly ever dream, but this one was as clear as day. It was the kind of dream that you fall back in to, maybe even a couple of times, and there are slightly different variations of the situation.

I hadn't had any dreams that I can remember since last fall, when I had a trio of nightmares involving a snake, a black widow, and a coyote. Those three dreams came consecutively, right after the job loss.

In the first dream, there were snakes slithering toward me, trying to draw me into the water. One bit me. I woke up in a fright. The next night, I saw a black widow in a web on the side of my kitchen island. I had to pass by it many times, and had to be careful not to come too close. But, it just stayed there—its fearful, lingering presence known. The third night, I was in a field, and a coyote started walking toward me. He was looking straight at me as he continued to approach. And then, he turned to the right and passed me by.

Any subconscious fear I was feeling about this change was subsiding; I was going to be all right.

This new, sweat-inducing dream was equally frightening, and interestingly timed. I had just got back from that glorious trip out east, so I was feeling quite rested, and I was enjoying some of the comforts of home, like my French press coffee. So, I was quite knocked off my feet with this unexpected dose of anxiety: I'm on a train, through the snow-filled tracks of Alaska. I've left the main car to take a jaunt to the bathroom and was amazed by the view: we were literally trudging through massive mounds of snow, so much so that I suspected in the dream that an ice breaker type apparatus must be on the front of the train to help us through. You could hear us crunching through the snow. I took a video and some pictures. And then I saw a clearing. We were slowly approaching a small village.

Then, almost instantly (as happens in dreams), I was outside of the train completely. In one version of the dream, I tried to take a picture from outside of the car, but the train jolted, and I fell to the snowy ground. I was stuck in this remote village, feeling afraid as I watched the train trudge on without me. After the shock subsided, I told myself that all would be ok—I was in civilization at least. It was unfamiliar territory but I would be able to do this.

In another version of the dream, I was back inside the train near the bathroom taking pictures. But instantly, there was an announcement that there was a lockdown: they were expecting an avalanche. Terrifyingly, I was alone and too far outside of the 'safe zone' to alert anyone to where I was. I was sure to be buried alive in the snow. I thought to text my eldest daughter, but realized I had no cell reception. I was trapped.

So I woke up wondering what all of this could mean, and some of the questions I asked myself were:

Am I feeling antsy because I have no clear goals? Do I feel like I'm being tossed aside? Am I feeling like I'm trapped, with little control? Am I feeling like I'm trudging? Am I not as settled with everything going on in my life as I think I am? What is going on?

Yes, I sometimes think too much.

And then I spoke with my tea-time friend who said, "Wait. Gareth *loves* trains. Maybe this means you need to get off his train."

[insert pause for moment of revelation]

That same afternoon, I spoke with my out-east-road-trip-friend. The conversation flowed quite directly to the dream. I wondered if I had had the dream because the entire year had been pretty much planned, and now there was nothing concrete in the horizon. I added that maybe the dream was related to how transitioning back from such a perfectly God-led trip was a little challenging; I had been noticing anxiety a lot more and had no tolerance for it. I also highlighted certain parts of the dream that I thought were interesting: being left behind, stuck, snow, train, fall, picture, alone, lockdown, locked, and avalanche.

Albeit comical, one of her first questions was whether I had considered the importance of the bathroom.

But it was a serious question.

What do I need to release?

How blessed I am to have so many amazing kindred spirits around me!

And then in entered a deeper wisdom:

Be assured that everything is on track. If you remove yourself from the situation and watch what is going on like you're watch-ing a movie—rather than being in the thick of it—you can better notice what's happening. This swirling is not of your making, or of your choosing. People around you expect you to get caught up in the storm—when it is not your storm—because there is a pattern there. In the past, you have rushed in, and tried to help.

Now listen. This will sound comical. You have a dog that needs to go out to relieve himself, yes? It would be interesting to collect it all in one bag for a week's time and keep it on hand.

And when a storm comes into the house, grab the bag, and put it on the table and say, 'Here. This is your bag of waste to deal with. I wish you well. I don't want to be a part of it anymore.'

It is a clear indication, and a marvellous visual of what is being done.

You need to detach. When someone comes in with their storm, stand above it. Of course they will try to project this storm on to you. You, yourself, have allowed this to be done before, more than once, and you've now reached the breaking point.

There was a re-awakening with the trip you took.

These people who bring in the storm are gifts to you, so you can better recognize when it's happening and learn to rise above.

You had to leave before (when you were the ripe age of 16). You did not believe you had the resources to survive without bumps in the road. There was a denial of self because you needed desperately to engage in survival. You had to put your dreams on hold to take care of necessities.

You were on the train of survival.

After the trip out east, you came back and you were re-aligned. Now, there is a blazing light shining out all that you are. You cannot return back to darkness after such a thing.

This is part of the transition.

Before, you were the responsible one. I say this softly because it was not that your husband did not work very hard, it was just that there was an immense amount of pressure on you. Perhaps the pressure wasn't felt so much for you because you liked what you were doing.

But now you see the contrast.

Most of your family members are old enough to make their way in their own choices. They don't need you to interfere, or to intervene.

For example, when you were out east, your oldest daughter dropped her cell phone into the ocean. This was a great lesson to see the impact of the story she told herself. The potentially ruined phone was the 'end of life'. It was a great drama. You stepped in with clear instruction on the steps to take. You did what needed to be done. The rest was hers. It was not your place to interfere. You encouraged her to let it be, that you've both done all you can, that all that was left to do was to trust. All that was needed was encouragement, maybe more than once because of her age, but that is all.

Your daughter with her phone is like some children that go through potty training. Some children are horrified because they think that what is in the toilet is part of them and if they flush it down, they will lose a part of themselves. They cannot see that there is a separation there.

Yes, this is a simple view of things.

Rather than intervening in others' lives, focus on *your* journey. There are residual emotions that need to be released. They are based on a lie that what has happened in the past will impact your future.

But that was then. This is now.

What you were feeling about what happened in the past was important to release.

Remind yourself that you are a holy being, that you are of tremendous value, and that you are beloved.

It is not your job to be the saviour of the world.

Your pattern—your design—is to make sure that you help others, and you are a peacemaker.

But this is detrimental to your wellbeing. You are upholding the responsibility of others at the expense of yourself.

Encourage yourself to look at what has happened in the past year. You were released from a job that you attached a value to. That is the con side. The pro is that it gave you a chance to use the many skills you were given when you were brought into this world to help others.

You don't throw this out because someone is feeling frightened.

In the past—indeed at a very early age—you had to put aside your playful side because there was a need within yourself to survive.

But that is not the case anymore.

You cannot let something go until you see it. So, now that you see it, as hard as it is for you, get off everyone else's train.

You do this by taking yourself away, like the people around you don't exist. You don't coddle them. You leave the car.

If there is an unpleasant situation, you have two choices. You can walk away, or you can sit there while the person flings their 'bag of negativity' at you.

And be cautioned to make sure that your own negativity doesn't cause harm to your home.

Kindly let the person know that they can have their temper tantrum. Tell them that you are there when they are done. Tell them that it is their choice what energy they bring into the room.

But rather than talking to them any more than that, talk to yourself, 'ah, someone isn't getting their own way and wants me to step in, but this causes me to get angry'. Don't step onto their train. Stay on your own train.

Theirs may be going over a cliff.

This dream is an excellent indication of the simplicity of what is happening.

Gareth is one of the trains. Being alone—off the train—you think put you in harm's way, but it is the opposite.

You saw on your trip out east how quickly you aligned with people who are light-hearted. You could feel how buoyant you became—because you fed off each other, you saw each other, you encouraged one another, you acknowledged how easy it could be: you remembered the truth of who you are.

You were out of your minds, so to speak, of how your minds were functioning for years. You re-aligned with source.

So stop the 'trainspotting': get off the Gareth train, the Naomi train, the Desi train, the this-train, the that-train, the trains of all those who attempt to impart upon you their opinions.

Your anger is within yourself. You have abdicated your own throne to create peace. You are creating disharmony in your own life.

There are wonderful things to explore. There are many things unfolding. It is uncomfortable, vulnerable, sensitive.

Let them each sit on their own bench for a while.

For example, shut the door of your daughter's messy room if it bothers you and if it bothers her, let her learn that if she wants it clean and if she wants to be treated like an adult, that her own hands make it so. It is in her own power to make it happen.

Human beings can create their own reality—it is where your power lies—you have the freedom to create what you like.

Even disharmony.

When you are in a storm of disharmony of someone else's making, let there be no shouting from you, just escape. There can be compassion and encouragement. You can say, 'I hear what you're saying but please excuse me. I know you will figure this out.'

For example, you can do nothing to deal with your husband's financial burdens. If you rush out to get another job, you will be dead in five years. Do not suppress your own heart's desires, or you will start to pinch yourself off from source energy.

Yes, human beings are unusual creatures in that you can create wonderful things. But, you can also create storms that draw you away from truth.

You are self-assured, and successful in experiencing the wonder of life. This creates discomfort for some because they cannot achieve this. It just has to do with the ability to tap into source energy.

On your trip, you felt it, and you mirrored it to others. There was a great sense of belonging, ease, and comfort.

Now, when you're in the presence of this not happening, there is a temptation to look for a way out. And it is through your invitation that it comes.

But this looking for a way out creates a distraction for you. You turn your back on the mountains of truth that are found in the situation. You deny the opportunities that these situations give you to realize, to remember, to learn.

You turn your back and run away from the truth that is right before you. Some turn to drugs, or drink, or new partners, or overeating. They are all things that numb the senses.

You believe that you are unable to keep your vibration up. So, to give yourself comfort, you anesthetize yourself; you try to escape—with alcohol, TV, the internet, or other things.

But you can do this same thing by changing your mind, by running, by taking a walk.

When you are in the midst of the storm, you can say softly, 'I see your pain. I hope this works out. All is well.' And leave.

Engaging in it is a distraction.

Your husband is worrying about this. You're worrying about that.

He is yelling this. You are yelling that.

In the end, you are both shouting the same thing. You are both bringing the same energy forward.

Stop.

Take a breath.

Excuse yourself.

Don't encourage bad behaviour.

Just leave.

But before you go, you can say, 'I can see I am bringing out the worst in you, so I will step away. Trust yourself that these feelings won't last long. You have the choice: go take a shower, and when you're done, come see me.'

Or, you have the choice to wallow with him. It may sound trite, but there are things you would rather be doing.

When you are in a storm—of your own making or another's making—ask yourself what thoughts do you have in mind? Will they leave you to increase the flow of life? Do they give you a sense of wellbeing? If not, take the opposite thought.

Just say, 'thank you for sharing, that's enough for now.'

You can call for help at anytime. You know this.

Don't go around cleaning up other people's messes, look at your own closet. It's a good scapegoat to get so involved with others. It's another way to numb the senses.

You can say that the rocks around your neck from helping others have prevented you from doing things you want to do in your life. But, my dear, the rocks are there because they are your rocks.

Engage in things that bring you joy. Lift yourself up and you will get to the point where solutions will come, my dear.

Speak from a place of truth, 'I find it difficult to be around you when you're acting like this.'

Compassion can come forth, 'I don't like being in that space either. Maybe you need to sit or take a nap. We are not alone. All is well.'

In doing this, the entire vibration changes.

Do not allow yourself to be in a box. You will not be happy there.

You have come too far forward in the light to be in darkness.

This is not to say that others do not have the right to act out, it just makes them less compatible.

Move on without carrying residual feelings. A relationship is not black and white where one person is bad and one is good. Remember that you have the same behaviours in you—you have had to give up to serve others—you have had to give up to belong.

And you can only give so much before the resentment rises.

You are here to expand the fullness of who you are. You don't have to stay hopeless and helpless.

Your heart's desire is to create wonderful things.

When you are out of alignment, you know it's wrong. It is not in keeping with who you are.

And, now that you've dug yourself out of the hole, your inner self is screaming, 'I will not go down into the hole again.'

You have had wonderful indicators of this. Your heart was literally broken. It doesn't get clearer than that!

When someone is acting out in front of you, say to yourself: 'There I am.

That is me.

But I don't have to stay there.

I don't have to surrender to this.

The goodness of life will take me away from this.

Ah yes! I know that peace.'

And you don't have to make them come with you on your path. You can bless them. When you are centred, you will know what to say. But keep it short, and leave.

Get off their train. It does nothing more than distract you from your own life.

Your road trip out east is likened to your lifeline. You came into your vehicle, and you drove through many places. It is like when you were born and grew up. As you went through life, there were new things to see, good experiences, food tastings, etc.

And then that 'chapter' of life was over. You came back to a different environment. You noticed things you truly enjoyed. You noticed things that were uncomfortable.

Any discomfort you felt was from past experiences and you picked it up and put it into the new 'life', or this new phase of your life.

This is like the journey through time—you get into the car, or the train, and you bring things with you. These things can affect your ability to understand your current situation.

When this happens, be cautious about any *strong* emotions. They aren't likely about the present time. It is very likely something in the past and you're over-reacting.

Just re-centre. This is present time. This is where you are now.

Remind yourself that it is a wonderful day. Today is a gift. Focus on the here and now.

What do you want to fill your day with? It is not your responsibility to fill others' lives. It is fine to give them options, but you need to take responsibility for the energy you bring to the present moment.

Don't feel too bad about yourself when residual emotions rise up, when the dial is dipping or moving toward the lower vibration side. It is your guidance system. It is an indication that there is a vibration that you are pulling yourself into. So you need to say, 'I'm not staying here. I'm pulling my train in another direction. I'll meet you at the next station, if you are there.'

In life, you go out and every day is a new adventure. On your trip, you simply changed the situation when you weren't pleased. You looked for opportunities.

You found divinity in the detours you took.

And now, you can look at it—that 'life line'—and you can see that now you are here. You can see this life clearer.

It is what you are writing.

And you will trust in the wisdom of your own soul.

And you trust that the wisdom of those you love will help them too.

It is not your responsibility.

You can go to the light.

You can refer *them* to the light.

But you are not going to have people veer you off course, so they feel better.

Take care of yourself, especially as a mother. The best thing kids can learn is to choose their inner world. If they are miserable, let them know that their energy is their own. It is best to leave them alone when they are wounded so they can learn how to soothe themselves and how to return to a place of peace. Or, they can choose to stew in it until they are like prunes. Either way, let them know that you are there when they are done and that you are always there to love them. And how quickly they will jump back into the light! It is typically faster for children because they are closer to the light than adults.

So get out into the sun. Take deep breaths. Take time with the flowers. Let them know how much you love and adore them.

To the grass that grows beneath your feet, to the trees that bow down to say hello, thank them for this gift.

And know that you can reach for more.

Life or Death

*You are not capable of carrying all
these rocks in your backpack*

When you hear that if you rush out to get another job, you will be dead in five years, it grabs your attention. It both confused me and caused me a little bit of anxiety.
So, I asked for more clarity on this topic.
And this is what I heard:

The first thing to address is delight with the joy experienced, which is accessible in any moment of your lives. It doesn't mean that you won't have the bumps in the road. It is an opportunity to learn the difference between the higher and the lower vibrations: and you have the chance to choose. Don't manipulate others to act a certain way, but focus rather on what to do about keeping yourself in the higher frequency.

The first one to speak about is regarding the work communication from before. It is not so much that you should not be working. You have many skills you have developed. It is a matter of trying to do the work with the rocks on your back that you don't want to carry. It is the stress of this, and the strain of trying to please those with expectations—those who express their thoughts about what you are doing—that weighs you down.

When you were the breadwinner, there was delight as it took the pressure off of him, but there was the resentment.

You carried this in your own being.

You carried this in your backpack.

You had this pressure that if you didn't do it, that things would go aground. You also had the pressure of wanting to be there with your children.

This split energy—of needing to be many places at one time—is what pulls someone down.

You cannot and you will not go back into this situation again. You have come too far. There is no worry about this happening again. But there is a little bit of knowledge required so you can delegate to others. You need to find the balance, and then the joy will be there.

Rather than responding with frustration to get something done—you can now give the information that you are not capable of carrying all these rocks in your backpack.

Be very clear that the right work will come along for you and your mate will make the necessary adjustments. He is willing to help yet he is not always knowledgeable of how to do it.

There is a great deal of self-doubt there.

When you work as a team, it will be a lot easier to accomplish goals, rather than fighting to breathe.

The removal of fear is the greatest thing that you can learn. You recognize when it is present, and you surrender it. Life goes on forever, there is really nothing for you to be concerned about.

You both have accomplished great things together—no pressure of mortgage—no pressure of debts—you are able to balance and keep things in alignment. The rest is just fear. Things work out for you—all is well.

You are responsible for taking care of your own fears. He is responsible to take care of his. There is no need to jump through hoops to make someone else feel better.

Just bring yourself back to the truth. It is quite simple.

It is good for you both to remember.

Now, another topic:

Each time that you come into a 'lifetime'—or a new chapter in your life—you are coming in specifically with a desire. There is something that you want to learn. And you have indeed learned a great deal on this trip regarding the flow with which life can be experienced. The trusting is a great thing that you have been able to see. And you are bringing what you learned out east into this new life.

As you move through life, you find that it just unfolds, rather than you having to make it happen. There is a plan for your life. There are many opportunities given in order for you to experience what you want in life.

Of course, free will comes in, and you have the choice.

The faith is strengthened. The strength is there. You see yourself guided and lead. This is what the trip was so good at showing. Indeed, there is power when two or more gather together[10]. For then you have the source energy very much in your viewfinder. When you can see the presence of God wherever you walk, you will see that life is a lot brighter.

Guilt, shame, and blame must be removed at all cost whenever you see that rise up and appear in your psyche. When you see it, you must replace it with the knowledge of who you are.

This is life or death, light or darkness, juxtaposed.

Honour your humanity, but know that you are created by love, for love, to extend love.

When you do feel bad, you can stop and ask yourself to forgive yourself. Remind yourself how beloved you are, and forgive yourself and let it go. The resiliency you see in your children is something to build within yourself.

And as you wake up in the new day, you move on. You remove the things from the day before, you look forward to what is waiting for you around the corner, and you move on.

Spend time in the meditative state and empty yourself out—and allow yourself to breathe in the good. Be in the moment—for that is where it all begins. Keep your mind on that which is good. Whether it be from the past, or from the future—or from the now—if you keep your mind on what is good now, you will always have that and good will come. Many times, the world will fill your belly with the 'to-dos' the 'might have dones' the 'oh my goodness, what is comings'. Empty that out, leave that baggage at the door, none of it is of any concern. It all works out. Just breathe in the light.

Envision the concerns as clutter all around you. Before you sit down, make a clear space within you, an empty space with which you can call in nothing else except life energy, the presence of God.

Thus, sit, and be still.

Shh—be still.

And soon you will find that the chaos will disappear.

And this you can do in the moment, in the midst of your hectic day, when you are busy. Take a moment to breathe in. Hold it. And breathe out. And remind yourself that there is nothing that can disturb your peace, when you make peace your focus.

Rather than 'I want peace,' tell yourself, 'I am peace. Peace is mine.' Then, you will shake off the concerns of the world for a good amount of time, if you allow yourself to do so. When you come back you will not find yourself in situations that are as stressful.

In that way, you will find that things get simpler, for there is a tendency for you to overcomplicate things.

Your trip was about this—you had to live very simply on the trip, versus all of the stuff at your home base. On the trip, you really had very little, yet you had enough—and it seemed to break things down so you could see the beauty in simplicity.

If there is too much stuff, if there are too many options, it gets too complicated. It gets hard to discern what it is that you are wanting—whether mental, or physical. It can impede the view and it takes you longer to make the decision.

That is why I say to keep everything simple—just keep your mind on everything that is good and look upon life with joyful expectation.

On the trip, you had the ability to see something that was not to your liking and just pivot. You didn't change what was happening you just adjusted. Simple.

You passed a certain site along the way and it was nothing. There was no urge to stop. But then on the way back, you passed that same site, and you lit up. You got the sign to stop—you followed it, you trusted it. Simple.

Be at peace with where you are: 'It is fine. It is ok.'

Very good.

Now, you are also asking yourself how you will know what is waiting for you.

But, you have answered your own question, my dear. In asking the question, 'how will I know?' you obviously know that you will know, when you know. It is like an admission of your ability to know what is in your best interest. You are one who will know—it will resonate on all sides—and you will know if it balances on all sides of your life.

Remember that you have had that sense of knowing many times in your life.

Trust the wisdom of your own soul, because it is very strong now. Remember, you can always ask, at any moment, for there is help available to you at all times from the prayers you send up, the requests for guidance. When you are uncertain, this would be the wise thing to do.

Ask for the help and spirit will guide you.

Sweet Nectar

People want to be a part of something delicious

It is uncanny that I currently have a stout in hand on an outdoor patio, and I'm listening to an unexpected acoustic guitar performance that just started up.

I'm absorbed in my inner world with external influence surrounding me. When I first got here, I could block out what was going on around me. But now, every single song that the band plays is a favourite of mine. I mouth the words to every song. It distracts me from my writing. It tempts me to lose my focus.

This seems fitting.

We distract ourselves. We numb our pain. We lose our focus. We fall into fantasy and illusion so very easily.

Because it feels *so* good.

I'm not being melodramatic.

In fact, the chorus of "Free Fallin"[41] is being sung at the moment. You gotta love Tom Petty.

You see, when the guidance came, I had two things in mind:

I recently was asked to do a consulting gig with an old-time colleague and it was splendid. I revelled in talking about an area I was passionate about for close to 20 years. It was three hours of bliss. I educated. I challenged. I stretched my mind.

My heart was happy. I smiled the entire way home. It felt good to share my acquired knowledge. But later that evening, part of me felt a bit of shame to feel this way. Was I selling out? Was I being tempted back into something that I was quite confident a few months ago was a done-deal?

I sometimes exhaust myself with over-thinking.

So I settled my thoughts by agreeing that it was ok to be proud of my acquired knowledge. There was no harm in remembering how intricate this niche area was, and how it fired up my brain.

Fair enough.

But, I opened my mind up to this and then two days later, I started getting heavily recruited for a job. A job they wanted to create for me.

Perhaps just coincidental, but the opportunity was tempting.

*

But in all fairness, the other thing that was still occupying a large piece of my mind was a wonderfully tempting proposition that came through via text while I was out east.

It started as an invitation to get together from an old acquaintance. I agreed and asked, albeit coyly, "What did you have in mind?"

While perhaps I had expected a slightly flirty response, I was not expecting the quite blatant response that came through. It was something like "I want you in my bed. I want to kiss you all over..."

I read those words more times than I care to count.

That same night, I had a stiff drink to calm my thoughts. And I went to bed hoping and praying for wisdom to come in the morning.

The next day, I took a deep breath—hoping to breathe in inspiration—and I texted back these words:

"I cannot be a conquest or merely conquest you.
It will harm my heart. It will steal my joy.
I can only share so much of it, my dear. You see?
It pains me to write this more than you know."
Then I deleted the entire message.

But I secretly wish I had saved his words. They were simply delicious.

And such things can linger in the mind long after.

And here is what I was given to ponder:

Words can be sweet or sour. But it is the intention behind the words that is important.

Are they words of encouragement and praise, merely stating gratefulness for your presence in their life, or is it said for other intentions?

Look as well on your perception of the words. 'Sweet' words that come from someone who you do not want affection from, have no attachment to them. They will just lay on the floor like a rug.

But someone can say sweet words to you and you can get caught up in them.

Don't get caught up in the words.

Because if you do, when someone gives you *sour* words— their opinion, their judgment, their criticism, or condemnation—it will crush you.

Thank the person for the sweet words. And, when someone has negative feedback, just thank them for expressing their truth.

The words are just simply what they are. They are words that are expressing the other person's vibration—it simply has to do with the other person and what their intent is.

When you give sweet words to others, you want to lift them up when they are in self-doubt. But, sweet words can also be manipulative. So, be discerning of the *intention* behind the words.

When someone comes to you with such a thing, it is always wise to take a look at why it has been drawn to you. The words that others say to you—whether sweet or sour—matter not, just focus on what you can do to extend love and joy into the world, my dear.

You get greater joy out of asking someone with negative energy to leave the room, or removing yourself from the energy, than standing there and letting it rain upon you.

You take greater joy by enabling someone to manage their own emotions, and see them strengthen that muscle, than watching someone be co-dependent. Is it not a feeling that is good when you extend knowledge that will help someone grow?

That same knowledge that you can give to someone to benefit them can be twisted. If the intention is for them to get the heck out of your way, the words may sound sweet, but the intention is not there.

So, you must always ask yourself, 'where am I in *my* intention on wanting to receive this?'

There are two parts of an equation. There is both the giver and the receiver—both have an intent on what the impact will be. It may be delivered from a manipulative tone—or not—only you can be the decider of which one it is.

Be strong and stable in what it is that you are wanting in your life. Right now, you are looking at the job, and the yoga. You are moving along with ease and flow. You feel good when your family life is strong. But none of these things will work if you are not doing what gives you light—when you give it and when you receive it.

For example, when you extend your knowledge to others (e.g. the consulting), it gives you light—it lights you up and it feels good.

Or, you take delight in a song and ask your guitar instructor to teach it to you and the excitement comes. You say 'I can learn this! This person can help me!' And you feel good—and the vibration rises.

And if the words are being given by this other one—and they are sweet words and they sound so lovely—if the intent, the cost of those words, is going to tear down everything that you are wanting, you need to ask yourself whether it will cause you moments of pleasure, and then hours of suffering.

So when someone meets you on your path, and gives you the sweet words, ask yourself what the attraction is. For that which you are trying to receive from another person is only what you cannot get from yourself. It is an indicator to yourself of what it is, you feel, that you are missing.

Let yourself be unburdened by the words that are running around, perhaps excitedly, in your head and your heart.

Just ask yourself why is it that you feel that there is this draw?

Have you been able to find it in yourself as to why this is so?

Let's play the 'let's pretend' game. Let's paint a whole picture: You come together. The sweet words become a sweet touch. The sweet touch becomes a sweet involvement. Then, there is a demand for more. And how is that going to benefit the life you have now?

How would that rest in your heart? Would that be a dark place for you or would it be light?

Perhaps initially, it is a bright place, because it is always very exciting when there is a coming together with a new energy. But all the while you are creating the dark place.

Moments of pleasure can become hours of pain that distract you from your desired path.

So always be aware of what your intention is. Some will keep you closer to God's love and some will draw you into darkness and fear.

The choice is sweet nectar or oleander poison.

Ask yourself whether this becomes another rock to tell yourself that you are not good enough. If so, this will only feed into the primal belief system that you have held in your heart: the lie that you are lesser than. And you have tried so hard and gone so far down the road away from that.

The true question is why the draw is there in the first place?

There are always feelings of self-doubt. People want to be a part of something delicious. It is the same for alcohol, food, drugs, success, the need for attention, praise, aggrandizement, or whatever you put in there that is tempting.

It all feels so good in the moment.

If food is the 'something delicious', the outcome may be extra pounds. If it is 'the need for praise', you may chase after it down a path that takes you farther away from where you want to go.

You have the possibility of the work, of the play, of the family, the children, the husband, the other possibilities...

You see? There is too much to work on.

And then comes the pleasure of distraction—this tells you clearly that you have taken on too much responsibility.

This draw has come to you in the first place because you are trying to run away from responsibilities that you yourself took on your shoulders.

You have wallowed around in a mess that someone else has made for you and now you realize that you want to focus on love and light.

That is what each of you is here to do: to service one another, to bring light and love so that peace can be found.

But for many, they spend their lives 'making sandwiches' for other people and never get the chance to live their lives. And then in comes the sweet temptation and it becomes problematic if too much time is spent focusing on it.

Live the joy of the moments of each day rather than being distracted away.

You are love, created by love, for love, and to extend love. It is your natural state of being.

And you may experience moments when the hose is wide open, if you will, and the love is flowing freely.

In these cases, it is a large figure eight. It is infinity; it goes around and around—it is strong and incredible—and you are so sensitive to it, and the world can feel it.

But it is not from another—it is from yourself and divinity.

Remember that there is no love but the love of God. You will never find it anywhere else. And the joy, the love (etc.) that you seek is already in your own being.

And once you realize that the love that you extend to another—that you seem to think is dependent on the person in front of you—is your natural state of being, it can never be threatened. It is not dependent on one particular person.

Once you realize this, it will flow freely. The only time it does not flow is when you hold fear as more dominant a vibration than the love vibration.

This is not an intellectual thing. It is a feeling thing. For many of you, it is hard to explain, but you know it when you feel it. You know when you are in the moment in front of someone (like when you did the consulting). You knew how you felt about the work. There was a vibrational thing.

You also know what it feels like when someone is in front of you screaming in your face. And you can choose one or the other. Shall I stay on a high-flying disc? Am I able to do this, or will I keep wallowing in the lower vibration in order to keep the lies that I have chosen to hold on to active?

When you leave this life, you will leave your body—and you will leave behind all of your earthly concerns. They will no longer exist and you will be unfettered by them. For when you come in to non-physical, you are absent from the body, present with the Lord[42].

It is all encompassing, all enfolding. All of these other things—this fear-based thinking, this resistance to love actively flowing through you—fall away.

And that is what you are each trying to do while you are here: to be able to hold much of that love, that vibration of love in your lives as you walk through this world.

No fear, no shame, no blame, no guilt, no feeling that you are not good enough. You are enough. The fact that you were born, that you were created, is enough.

And when you have that in your heart—when you know this truth—you will then be able to look at the other one who comes with the sweet words and say to yourself, 'Those are sweet words. Isn't it nice to hear sweet words' and you will not question what it is they mean, and why they are there. You will be able to take those sweet words and just enjoy them.

And you will not necessarily need to go into your mind and think about action.

It is like walking by a garden. You see a beautiful flower. You smell the beautiful fragrance. And how lovely it smells! But, you don't need to pick the flower. You can enjoy the deliciousness without having to make anything of it. You just enjoy it and on you go.

The long and the short of all this is don't make too much of it.

So take a deep breath. Take your shoulders down from your ears, and be reminded that all is well.

All is well.

You are one who is surrounded by much love. Do remember this when you are making your choices.

And, do remember that you all have the assistance of the light available to you. It is always there for you. You can call on it at any time. It is a mere ask away.

Opportunity Knocked

It is the absolutes that will stop you in your tracks

So the consulting gig started when an old colleague contacted me wanting to pick my brain about an investment idea he was looking into. And as I mentioned earlier, I delighted in the fun and allowed myself to let the feeling linger.

Then I found myself in an interview room that went entirely successfully. It was a slam-dunk. There was passion, and excitement. It rendered a smile in my heart. They wanted to create a new senior position for me. How much of a compliment was that?

And then the final interview was done and I had nothing to do but wait.

I found it interesting to think about the timing of all of it. I had said that I would be taking at least a year off. And that year was coming to an end.

I also found it thought provoking that this potential new beginning was almost like a full circle back to where I started.

Which I didn't necessarily think was a bad thing.

Because now, I was feeling much more grounded.

But my belly was telling me otherwise. Despite the positive attitude, I found myself launching into a barrage of, 'but-I-thoughts...' and 'I'm not readys.' I had debates like, 'I don't want to fall back into old habits' versus 'I think I've come far enough along that it won't happen' and 'I'm concerned that it might be difficult to stand my ground' versus 'I will find the time to do what's important to me' and 'But the consulting meeting was so fun, maybe I should open up a consulting business?' versus 'I thought God had a different plan for me—a new life—a completely new focus—but maybe that was just my own ego talking?'

A friend of mine recently asked me whether I always think so much.

It's a fair question.

Opportunity knocked, and I wasn't sure if I wanted to let it in.

But I did know that I desperately wanted the cerebral, logical, data-driven, back-and-forth incessant analysis, and inner dialogue to stop.

And despite the guidance I had received thus far, I was still having a hard time just letting go, and just letting it be.

And then more wisdom came:

You are very good at processing at this point in your life. Indeed, there are two contrasting vibrations that you can see very well and you are very good at working within them. But, what is coming through are the absolutes. And, it is the absolutes that will stop you in your tracks.

When you are speaking about the work you have done for many years, you found yourself lighting up, as though you had taken the dimmer and turned it into a brighter light. This is a wonderful feeling and lets you know that you are on target, and that you are enjoying what you want in life. When you are thinking of these things, it brings you those good feelings.

This is an area in your life that gives you light: to be of service, to navigate through this world, and help others to navigate through. This gives you satisfaction.

There is no need to diminish the light you see in this. It is a wonderful thing.

What is coming through in the rest of it is fear-based thinking. The what-ifs, the buts, the sos, and things like that.

You did a great amount of work to bring yourself into great joy with the yoga experience. You take great delight in this.

You also take great delight from your children and from your husband when he is not in fear-based thinking himself.

So here comes the opportunity for you to possibly re-enter the work place, where your energy will be focused on what delights you.

It is the self-imposed lie working in your belly that says you cannot go and enjoy something for yourself. It is an untruth to think that you are not free to do this unless you know that there are no other catastrophes around.

This is not a negative thing.

It is a wonderful indicator to be able to see. The fact that you are no longer willing to take responsibility for things that they, themselves, are responsible for, is wonderful.

They were baiting you in—and you were floundering in the pool—and you are not willing to do this any more.

You are on a trajectory, a path that you have carved out for yourself that gives you great delight. And then someone comes along and starts to reel you off course by calling for help. That gives you the opportunity to choose—or not—to go off your path.

But you do them no service to run and help them for the 100th time.

This is where there is a duality. Your energy is split. You have taken too much responsibility upon yourself.

Regarding the absolutes, hear it clearly—and have it as a banner before you—that when you step out on the path, when you make a choice, and you think it is not a good choice, you can simply make another decision.

It is as simple as that.

But what happens is that you put things in your own mind. You may say, 'I've made a wrong decision', 'I've done harm', or 'oh silly me'...If you paralyze yourself with fear, you lose the here and now, and the beauty of the moment you are sitting in.

In your situation now, look at what it is that delights you. Perhaps you say, 'I have great knowledge in this area. I do not find this difficult. I enjoy the contribution I make. I enjoy the husband when he cares for himself. I like the yoga. I like when the children are at peace, and have the opportunity to learn that they create their own reality from the mental choices that they make. I like it when these things happen.'

You like a home that is neat and orderly. You like it when you can reach for something and find it, and knowing that when you put something away it will stay put. You delight in this, rather than running around in the organization that slows the task at hand.

It is the peace you seek after.

Now, if you look back on this past year, you will find there has been a tremendous amount of growth in the area of clarity.

The life journey has come with a lot of loose ends. And this year has allowed you to get a clear perspective on what you are wanting, desiring, and what lights you up. And it has allowed you the opportunity to find the clarity, and feel deserving of receiving all the wonderful things that you enjoy.

And it is the *deserving* component that you have been working on in this past year. Not the absolutes of 'I must get this right.' You have come to the realization of knowing what it is that you want in your life, and you receive it.

Understand fully that the blessings are always there—it is whether or not you feel deserving to receive them.

As you have come closer to the knowledge of divine light, that you allow to manifest in your world, you have been able to find peace.

And, yes, you want it for everyone—but they will find it for themselves.

Keep going. Tell yourself regularly, 'things always work out for me. God loves me and cares for me and is bringing wonderful things.'

Remind yourself that God has a plan for you. Ask, 'what would he have me do on this day?'

Ask divinity what will bring light into this world.

Keep your focus on the possibilities. Gather the information, as you have, of what is required for the job and ask if it is what you are wanting. There will be a shift in the dynamic, to be sure. But you can set it up so that you can get some if not all of what you are wanting.

And also, take the word 'don't' out of your language. 'I don't want...' The word 'don't' isn't heard. The only thing that is heard is the subject matter.

It is like someone who says, 'I don't believe in God,' but the moment they speak the word, he is in the room.

Try to keep the language on what you are wanting—and you will bring those things into manifestation and into focus.

'I'm wanting you to come to know how capable you are,' versus 'I don't want you to put this burden on me.'

'I want you to trust your instincts,' versus 'I'm not wanting to do this for you.'

Once you release all of the 'don'ts' that you have in your mind—the job, the yoga, the children, the family life, the relationship with the husband, the health/wellbeing, the other relationships—everything will become easy.

Joyful expectation is the focus on receiving these wonderful things.

Also bear in mind that the nature of human existence is that you will always have troubled times wherever you go. There will be moments of discontent, frustration, questions of whether you are on the right trail.

And that is ok.

It is not a matter of trying to stop the questions coming. You hear yourself ask these things, and there is nothing wrong with you. It is just a clear indicator that you are processing.

Just avoid lingering there in that vibration.

The how will present itself. The first step is to be strong in vibration regardless of what is going on.

Once you hear God as you are sitting quietly, once you become so familiar that it is the only voice you hear, then you will know the how.

You have been strengthening your attunement.

You already come as a bright light. You shine so brightly that you are able to shake yourself off and get back on the path because you have the desire to do so and your love light is too strong to be swayed.

Immerse yourself in joyful expectation for the next moment.

You are doing better than very well. Keep attuned to God, my dear.

All of you have the capacity to do this. You are all connected. You have the opportunity to help those who haven't learned. And it is in the teaching that you learn. And you always have the assistance of the light. God will give you the resources to bring it into fruition. When in doubt, turn inward.

When you stay focused on what it is you want, you will have clarity. It will never be serious like a concerning brow. It will be a 'how would you have me handle this?'—a lighter vibration.

Don't be worried you won't get it right. Just follow the prompting you have right now. It takes the tension off.

Whatever is on your plate for the day will lead you and it will appear in front of you.

It is not incorrect to be impatient because the excitement is there—the 'I can't wait to see where this is going!'

Love the impatience. Love the anxiousness. They are precious, they are important. You are doing well.

The trip brought you a great deal of synchronization, a great deal of clarity, and a deeper sense of peace in what you are doing.

This is why your writing has increased so much for there are many perspectives and stories in your being that will help uplift others.

This isn't new. You have had the impulse to write for many, many years.

But you have not yet graduated from this course.

Your greatest gift is your ability to draw things out of people, to help lift them up to the truth of who they are. It happens wherever you go, in the gas station, in the grocery store, with your family and friends, with your work mates, etc.

When you are attuned with God, you have a light that blazes in you, without a word.

So, just stay focused on each moment. Be true, steadfast and let your light shine for others.

They will then see their light reflected back in them.

How wonderful is that?

Heads or Tails

You are learning to flip the coin on its head

Having kids gives you a chance to have old childhood stories ringing in your ears.

One story got me to thinking:

The three little pigs grew up and went out to make houses for themselves. As the story goes, one made a house of straw and another made a house of wood. The last—the wisest of the lot, as the story goes—made his house out of brick. So, when the big bad wolf came, all the pigs were safe in the strong brick house. There is a lesson to be told here: taking the time to build a strong foundation, and having solid support around you is really important.

No disagreement here.

However, building brick walls can have some drawbacks...

Consider this: you get a little older and you meet someone and fall in love. The two of you are inseparable. At the beginning, it's easy to see that you're lovable. You don't have to bring out your scars and your wounds. But, we are all imperfect humans. Our insecurities, fears, past hurts will come out at some point in time—we can only hide them away for so long.

Don't you wish that you could throw them under the rug and be done with it?

But those fragments of our past, those dirt-filled areas that we don't even want to think about, build up over time and that accumulation of soot starts to show. So before things get too messy, we start building up our protective walls.

Your first fight lays the first brick down. You get criticized and embarrassed, with witnesses! [brick] You get interrupted for the 100th time [brick]. You get contradicted...again [brick]. You just can't seem to meet expectations [brick]. You get in a few more fights [brick]. You don't feel supported [brick]. You have visitors arrive who were invited over for dinner without your knowledge [brick—ok maybe more than one]. You get yelled at [brick]. You yell [brick]. You go out for dinner, and are ignored the entire time [brick]. You get stood up and you find out later that you were just completely forgotten about [brick].

And before you know it, you have a pretty good partition around you. If you keep going, you might get a good, solid house built around you: one that the big bad wolf will never get in.

But no one else will get in either.

And then, in came the deeper wisdom:

The perspective that you are looking at these situations is coming from an earthly position.

There is a deeper thing going on.

Everything that comes up in your experience, gives you the opportunity to identify it as darkness or light. And some things pull us closer, and other things push us in a direction away from 'unity to the light.'

The freedom that each individual—each man and each woman—has the ability to experience in their lifetime has boundaries set by the particular society that they are in.

It is like there are only two choices: heads or tails.

And, the separation between man and woman has become greater.

There has been a shift in the frequency on this planet.

There is less tolerance—in the relationships you will encounter with friends and family, and the roles of the man and women—because the soul is being called to that place of authenticity.

And, you cannot be authentic when you are working toward the needs of others.

There has been an oppression of the female and children, in the society of men, and humankind.

The desire for growth and expansion is so great. You come to grow, expand, and experience the deliciousness of life. You cannot do this when given belief systems that will restrict your movement or your thought patterns.

The female side of the human kind has to be able to flow in and out. And with each generation, this is becoming increasingly visible. That is why you are seeing tremendous resistance to the violence in this world, and other things that are not keeping with health and wellbeing.

You tend to have the restrictions imposed on you by your family of origin, and societies, which is in contrast to what you know in your authentic being. You know something is out of whack, out of alignment, and you struggle with this, when you come to this place—generally in your thirties—when you realize your mode of operation is not giving you what it is that you are wanting in life.

So then you start to move toward what the other way could be. You start to expand and grow, and learn healthier concepts that give you a sense of creativity and balance—and a higher worth, vibration, frequency—than that which has been holding you in bondage.

And this is why you are seeing it in those around you. And this is not necessarily that the male is in the 'bad guy' role. They are taught by society to behave in a certain way because the man will want to dominate and the woman will want to cooperate. It is the role that has come down through generations, time and time again.

This is why when you—the female aspect—are more willing to step aside to accommodate, you have a hard time breathing.

There has been so much mental noise, and it has happened so many times, that there is a little death each time—and it becomes unbearable.

So you want to get away so you can hear your own inner voice speak.

You are all longing for the carving out of space for one's self to be able to breathe deeply, to move freely, and to allow spirit to move through you.

As females, you are more able to see the connection to yourself and spirit, for you are built—physiologically—to be able to carry children in your womb, and give birth.

And because of this, it is something that comes more naturally. The familiarity of being focused on inclusion is a far greater vibration for the female than the male. The *need* is not true from a biological perspective, but it has been imposed upon the female in a societal way; for a woman who does not think of others is often cast in a dark light.

So, as a female, you may feel it sooner and at a greater depth than the male incarnate. This is a concept that is more difficult for the male to understand because it is not done at such a cellular level. And, the male still needs to keep within the safety of the confines set for men: this is how men are 'supposed' to behave, to think, and what they are supposed to do.

It is an antiquated system.

In the last few decades, it has been moving toward a freer concept.

However, it is still a little bit like a crustacean trying to take off the shell; there is a resistance on the part of the male.

This is because they have had more of the personal freedom than the female has, and they are not willing to give it up. Or rather, there is reluctance, for there are some who are giving it up freely.

For you are all being called—male and female—to a higher vibration.

Divinity calls everyone.

Rejoice—all of you—that you are finally able to lay aside the guilt, shame, and blame of not being everything to everyone and you are more willing to embrace spirit as it moves through you.

You will be the ones, as females, to reach for the light more than anything else. You will make it a priority. You are feeling this.

You understand this.

We feel that you are doing very well in your connection, and you are intuiting many things.

Let everything that you are doing, my dear one, come from the place of joy.

It is the joy you are missing when you are being interrupted by your children. Even though they are young ones, meaning no harm, interruption is interruption. And, it is the interruption of being lit up that can 'turn the lights off'.

Understand that these little ones are in the flow. They are filled with spirit and bounce from this to that. When they are interrupted, they don't feel a threat from it. If something upsets them, they simply need a bit of soothing, and they are right back. They are buoyant. This is their nature. And it is lovely.

But as you grow older, you don't flow as easily. You don't bounce as freely because you hang on to things and the rocks around your neck weigh you down. So interruption becomes a threat. You build expectations and have the thought that interruption is a bad thing, so it distracts you.

It is a 'so what' and a 'what is so'. For example, it is raining. Are you making a big deal of this or is it not a big issue because you're inside?

Listen to your intuition, for you have a good connection there. And, the more detachment you have from the ways of the world, the clearer the communication.

The more practice, the clearer the receiver.

It is very easy for you to become so easily meshed into the ways of the world—as you were taught to relate to it—that you are unable to recall the truth of who you are.

Now you are learning to flip the coin on its side; you are able to identify the truth of who you are. You have knowledge and wisdom that you can accept only when you give up the thought that you are separate.

The human part of you is a very small aspect of you, but it dominates your consciousness, because you have been taught not to see anything else.

Yes, the ego is a *part* of the human experience, however the level to which you identify with the ego will dictate the way you walk in the world. That is, if you are thinking that your ego is you, you will remain attached to the ways of the world.

You have that identity of 'I am this,' and 'I am that' and you think that that is who you are. And then one day you have a strange and unusual experience that seems to give you the idea that there is more to the picture than you think. And once you have that moment of being aware—the slightest inkling of the fullness of who you are, even the slightest crack in the door— you will know that you are more than the ego.

It may be a simple statement like, 'there must be more to life than this.'

And you start to experience the other aspect of yourself. You become aware of the still small voice.

Source energy did not just plunk you here and abandon you. You came in with that connection to source.

However, you were taught to deny that aspect of yourself and trade it in for the new mode of operation handed down from generation to generation. That gives you a limited view.

It is similar to going to another country, and knowing only one thing about the place. When you arrive there, you find out that what you were told is in direct contradiction and you have to make the adjustment.

And you find that where you are going is far freer, brighter, and joy-filled than what you were told.

As you become more aware of the truth of who you are, and more willing to move through this life from the position of knowing who you are—it is like exercising a muscle—you become stronger.

When you feel spirit move through you—when you allow this to take place—it becomes something you want to happen more. You start to practice it more in your life and this new way of looking at the world becomes part of you.

It infiltrates the way that you look at things through your eyes. You detach from the old systems and open your eyes to seeing life through a different lens. It is as simple as this.

As you become more willing to abandon your belief systems, you are able to translate quicker and easier.

And this happens with all of you. You become more proficient to translate the words that flow through you.

This year, when you have had to move aside from the fear and the uncertainty—and no longer having the role you used to—when you were able to release that baggage, you were able to hear and translate that which you were always in touch with.

For, in the past, you had the voices of others in your head that were dominantly directing you.

And the more delighted you became with the experience of being able to do the writing and having it flow more quickly, the more you decided to do it, and the healthier your body was to respond to it.

Indeed, it is a delight to see the joy—to feel the vibration rise in you—when you are standing in the light.

Trailblazer

All you have to do is follow the breadcrumbs

And then, I found out that the creation of that senior position was not meant to be.

The hiring manager called me himself and shared that he was frustrated and disappointed. He gave me the most glowing review of my skills that I hung up the phone and felt so good, that I could hardly muster up any negative emotion.

Admittedly, I was a tad confused, because I had really tried, over the previous weeks, to wrap my head around going back to work. I reminded myself of the positives of going back to the corporate world so many times that I thought I had started to believe them.

But mostly, I was relieved that this wasn't my time.

Despite my conscious attempts otherwise, I might have willed this not to happen through my unconscious fear.

And this just made the story more interesting: it was a 'plot twist'.

But my husband, deep in his heart of hearts, wasn't as reassured as I was.

And, perhaps it was coincidental, but he was now in a state of panic and said some things that he shouldn't have said.

And while the details of what he said don't matter, and his immediate regret was evident in his eyes, he still had gone too far.

His words had crossed a line, and he was too difficult for me to be around.

Each of us had some things to sort out on our own.

So, I made a few arrangements for the girls to stay with relatives, I packed up some things, and I tucked myself away at my parents' cottage up north.

Along with my yoga mat, and my guitar, I brought up my sewing machine with the materials to finish the t-shirt quilts that I had been working on for my girls for a good long while.

I stitched together these little square memories of time gone by—these pieces of shirts and dresses that they wore close to their hearts—collected for as long as I can remember.

I was holding the same fabric that rubbed against me when they were young, as I hugged them, and comforted them, and loved them.

And here I was—in stark contrast—alone.

But this wasn't entirely a bad thing.

This was a rare chance to get away to somewhere calm, to realign.

And I had planned to come up north a few weeks earlier, but the final interview for the job got in the way of it.

So, while many tears were shed thinking about the upsetting words that followed me from home, on with this creative task I went, listening to old CDs that I found in a cottage cupboard.

And two solid days later, I carefully folded up the ready-to-be-quilted projects and brought them in to the closest town's fabric store.

I walked in and spoke with the owner. I had my fingers crossed, so to speak, that she would take on the job because some of the square pieces had jewels on them and some were filled with sequins. Other areas had thick embroidery on them and one square had a flower sticking out at least an inch. So, quilting it on a long-arm was not going to be an easy task.

In fact, I had one store tell me that they wouldn't touch it with a ten-foot pole.

So with a hopeful heart, I pulled out my youngest child's quilt and laid it flat on the table.

It was then that tears started to well up in my eyes. This was a project that I hoped and dreamed about doing for almost as long as my children have been alive. There never seemed to be enough time.

But now, overwhelming gratitude washed over me as I realized that it was now coming close to the end.

And then this stranger took her hand and touched one of the squares with a kitten-in-a-tutu on it, and smiled. She lovingly ran her fingers down the quilt, examining the sashing, and the stitching, and perhaps trying to make sense of what the memories were. She stood there doing this for a good while. She then spoke aloud all that I didn't know I needed to hear. She said something like "What a lovely thing you have done. What beautiful memories this will be. You did such wonderful work. Well done."

At least a tear or two fell in that store.

And, I carried a piece of her gentle-heartedness back with me to the cottage.

So now, with a clear head, and an open heart, I opened up my laptop computer, took a deep breath, and captured this guidance:

You did not sign a contract that said that you would be the one to take on the role of primary responsible.

By leaving, you have taught yourself that when someone throws their negative energy your way, it is not your job to pick up the mess.

You have been trying to make sure everyone is happy first before you do what makes you happy. And, your inner child is weeping because she's not being taken care of.

But, this time you made a choice for light.

Your husband is not used to taking so much responsibility, and you have been doing it long before you should have been.

You're being prompted to do something. You had that same desire in you when you did your master's degree. God doesn't give you desires unless he wants you to follow through on them.

When you have to turn these desires off to compensate for others, you know it's wrong in the depths of your soul and you have to remind yourself of this.

Your plate was so full it almost killed you.

But now you say, 'You've gone too far.'

Now you say, 'Take your fear and come back here when you're done.'

Now you tell him, 'The problem isn't that you're scared. You're allowed to be scared. The issue is the projection coming on to me, that if it wasn't for me, you wouldn't be afraid.'

This is an illusion. It's not reality.

But it works because it takes the responsibility off of him.

He is stepping out of light and in to fear.

What you have been trained to do is to go into the darkness with the person and drag them out. But, you momentarily lose connection—you push source energy out of your life—in the moment that you dive into the darkness.

It works to stay in the light and call the person forward to you.

So you need to make a choice. What kind of life do you want? Yes, you may need to make a few little adjustments, but these are wee little things. Catastrophizing these things is just playing mind games—and when you do this, you're not aligned—*you* have gone too far.

Let it go. It's that simple.

Because, when the darkness and the fear, and the worry and the upset, and the panic are in the forefront, it puts the entire family on unstable ground. Rather than focusing on the light, and the hearts' desires, and the loving, and the looking forward to, now everyone is focusing on what the outcome will be of this bad behaviour.

And, this is where it becomes destructive.

It is wrong for anyone to support a person to stay stuck in his head. It's like enabling an addict that goes to the unhealthy place. They need to learn that this action brings about a certain consequence.

For you, yourself, have learned how strong the impulse is for you to work on your inner world, so you do not get caught up in it.

When you are called to write, it is a joy-filled experience. It is not a drag. So when someone tells you to go in another direction so it is easier for them, what does that accomplish?

You have to do what you are called to do.

And, that is probably why the other man comes to your mind—and brings to you words of appreciation and delight. No wonder you want to go there.

So, do exactly what you did: state your ground and state it clearly: 'I don't want to be the target of your outburst. I'll go away. My legs work fine.'

And do not let your own fear-based thoughts get in the way—'If this doesn't work, my only option is that I'm going to have to move. How will this affect the kids?'—rather than doing things that give you joy.

You can also go through simple worst-case scenarios by saying calmly: 'I can see you're really frightened. Why don't you go back and live with your parents and I'll go to the welfare office and explain my circumstances. You keep doing your job and live rent-free and you won't have to worry about us.'

Or, 'Why don't I go back to work and get so stressed out that I have a heart attack and you can have it all? How does that work for you?'

It's ok for him to be afraid. But it's not ok for him to be projecting this on you. If this is the result, one of you needs to remove yourself from the situation.

Which is exactly what you did.

And the trip you went on did the same thing: it was an opportunity to see how God can work through your life when you give it up and let him be your 'trailblazer'. Everything was effortless.

All you have to do is follow the breadcrumbs and the display is unfolded in front of you.

You are very good at knowing what you need to do. Have a good cry. Don't get too much in your head. Let it go. Set the tone. Hope and pray that you can have the space required to complete what it is that you want to do.

In the past, you have taken yourself out of joy and distracted yourself.

It is easy to do.

But now, it is a delight to see how you are sorting things out, and bringing through the knowledge. It is the non-physical side of you, the non-consciousness, who is speaking to you. And then words are coming to you. That is the gift. And after that, whatever is going to transpire will flow. Allow that flow to continue to come through and trust it.

It is like the choice that you made between staying in the darkness of the mud puddle and taking yourself away to stay in the light.

If you are in a relationship, it's like you're working as a team.

You have the belief that your survival is dependent on the equilibrium in your relationship. If one wheel goes off, you feel that the entire vehicle will go in the ditch.

It is like the other person is responsible for your safety in some way. So, you project that they need to behave in a certain way in order for you to survive.

And when they get out of alignment, they come at you and project their fear.

Then, you project your fear back.

It becomes a dance of fear.

But, none of that would be at play if you held on to the truth.

They have a whole story in their minds that is based on fear and it needs to be removed, which is why they come to you: to help them get it out of their head. It's their story.

If you come back with the truth—'There is nothing to fear', 'God provides, he has always provided', 'We have never had to worry about this' etc.—if you're standing in the strength of that truth, you cannot be wavered.

What you do, it seems, is when they come in with their story—with that 'truth'—you buy in to it, instead of countering it. You have a seed in your own mind that it might possibly be true.

Their fear is financial or feeling too much pressure. Your fear then is that you're not able to do what you want to do—that you feel called to do—because you have to take care of the storm.

You don't have to engage in that. You can recognize it as *their* storm, not yours. Knowing there is a storm, you can acknowledge it and you can say something as simple as: 'I hear you. I'm sure you're able to take care of this. You've dealt with this before.'

But what you do is you push back. You say, 'get this energy out of my face. Do not come at me with this!'—because you have it in your head that this person, as your spouse, cannot speak to you or react to you that way.

But, they can do whatever they want to. They can scream and yell at anyone. They have the freedom and the free will to do this. If it were a stranger doing it, you would just remove yourself. But, because it's your spouse, an indignance comes up—'how dare you speak to me like this?'

This is hostility right back.

So remind yourself of the truth: there is no threat. It is just discomfort from the noise.

And just remove yourself. Like hail coming from the sky— you can stand and get hit on the head or you remove yourself. You don't get angry at the hail for falling down on you.

There is a difference between looking at something and knowing you can make a choice versus feeling like you have nothing to do other than face a barrage.

If you do walk away from the situation, you don't have to leave by kicking sand in their face and with hostility. You can just walk away.

Forgive them; they know not what they do.[43]

What destroys you is the energy that you throw back.

It is what pains you the most.

It doesn't mean that the other person is right or wrong. Anyone can choose their own behaviour, but how long before you take care of your own inner child? How long do you allow yourself to placate this way—this inner child that has had to be put in a room, out of harm's way and ignored—to take care of another person?

This distracts you from doing what it is that you want to do.

You do this because of a lie that, 'this is my spouse and I am responsible for their happiness.'

But, you are not.

You say, 'I do this to keep this all together.'

But, no, you are not responsible for how another person responds.

Sharing burdens with one another is ok. But taking care of their things is not. When they get out of alignment and they come at you, be clear, with a touch of encouragement: 'You will figure this out. Don't throw it all my way.'

They can take it to God. That's the opportunity. Tell them that, 'God is the only one who can help you with the story you have created in your head. Take it to him.'

Be in the company of those who are behaving in a godly fashion—your cloud of witnesses—because when people come to you with their darkness, you can lose this.

And, there are no more minutes to lose in that kind of energy.

You have enough to deal with—with all that is swimming around in your own head—to be able to deal with someone else's illusions.

Remember that removing yourself from negative energy allows you to realign; to reconnect with source energy; to return to a state of calm; and to be reminded of your path.

And, divinity—this source energy—is not out there for only *certain* people. It is not out there *externally*.

It is available to all of you.

It resides inside of you.

Truth Serum

This is the freedom that needs to be passed on

And when I write, I feel the words flowing through my heart, and my mind; they run from the tips of my toes to the crown of my head. They follow me along my travels.

Now, they are my constant companions.

But I am still an interpreter; I don't want to get it wrong.

I don't want to risk messing up such a sacred thing, because words are complex and wonderfully good, but they can also be negatively connotative.

So, I tell my story and let things flow, but at times I still worry: 'Am I doing this right?'

I try not to get caught up in these fear-based details, and wisdom tells me the same:

You are sensitive to the feelings of others, which is good. But what you are writing now is for *you*, indeed. You are telling the story to the child.

This child is you.

This child is in all of you.

There is the truth of who you all are. And, there is the self you need to be to live in this world—the movement of keeping oneself as part of the herd. Sometimes this consideration can become so great that you trip over yourself.

You alone know when you are doing this.

It is not a bad thing to think 'what will be acceptable for others to hear?' and 'how can I say this in a way that will not cause too much discomfort for another?' These are all good things.

However, at this point in the game, it is not important. For now, just write it down. You are not alone when you are doing the writing. You have the assistance of the light with you.

It is so good that you can write and discern, and distill it down so it is quick and easy for people to grasp. You have a gift with words, which is why you have the urge to get these things out.

It is the love you have for others that is getting you to do this.

This is what is propelling you forward. By expressing the shifts and the changes in the landscape of the inner world—as you are moving through these experiences—it will help others do the same.

So just take this information and write it down. There is no need to see how it would be directed. There is really no need to put these questions at the beginning of the process, because it will limit you.

Just write about what is in your heart.

Write your truth, fully.

And when you have enough, everything will come together.

This doesn't mean that you need to share all of it with the world, but rather to start by writing it all down first.

If there are parts of the story that are a part of others' stories (e.g., a childhood experience), and you have it in the back of your head that, 'I can't really say this', you jump ahead and you start to edit, instead of telling the experience. This is why you need to tell yourself at this point that this is for you. Tell the journey to yourself. Be fully honest about the concepts, the gems, and the growth of the experiences. Write it all down. Do not censor it according to how you think it *should* be done, or concern yourself with getting the chapter perfect.

Do not limit yourself, or concern yourself with what anyone else will feel. Just get it down.

You cannot do this if you are working within the world and what is expected.

It will limit you.

Indeed, do not get pushed into anything, but do not push things away either. Just put them in the pile of possibility, it's that simple.

It takes the pressure off, like a joyful game.

Later on, when it is the time—and this doesn't mean when you are 80 years old—when you feel that the particular theme is complete. Then, read it, and re-read it. Then you start to edit it and mould it into the final product. This is when you will reach into that pile, and you will choose. And you will put the final dressing on these words that have come through you.

Indeed, you will take each word and put it in its finest clothing before you let it out the door.

You do not need to worry about how to put it out there. It is not a requirement right now. For the present time, the work is to let it flow and enjoy the deliciousness of it.

This is a gift for you. The self that you speak to is the self who will pick up the book and read.

This is why the books that you yourself have read you say, 'ah, this person has been walking with me.'

It is because the attunement is with every person who is walking this earth.

Each one of you has a gift to bring to the world.

When you start telling your story and giving it out as a gift, you are giving your heart out, as you say. You are asking the reader to be kind, to accept it and to receive it, if they see themselves in this. Perhaps it will help them with the bumps in the road and help them with their journey.

Let it flow, dear one.

You do not have to be concerned about time. There is no time limit with which you need to complete it. And it will take longer to complete it if you are caught up in the mud of what is acceptable. Blow out those boundaries—take the fence away and let the horses run free. Let those words run freely.

And then, later on, as you start to 'edit', that is when you are bringing the words to a place where they are more digestible for the masses.

Where the truth of what you wanted to say has been sculpted in such a way that when those who are meant to read it know exactly what is being said, and they will relate to it. And they will relate to you. And the words on the pages will resonate strongly.

That will be the end product—you have no need to be concerned about that.

Not to belabour it, just be clear on this point.

Most of you walk through this world, and you are walking with this voice on the shoulder that tells you that you must please others, that you must get it right, that you must shape and mould yourself in order to fit in to what the desires of another person is.

You second-guess.

So you don't let your light shine. You sort of let it lighten in some areas, but you dim your own light; that light that sparks in you, you dim down in order to make others feel more comfortable.

In some situations, this is fine to do—to meet people at their vibration. You cannot have someone understand a language they have not yet learned.

The vibrational frequency of someone who has never loved another human unconditionally—how do you expect them to know what you are talking about? If someone has never been on a bike and felt the wind on their face, how would they know how that feels?

If someone has never gone on a wonderful trip like you did—your excitement will make them want to smack you in the face. They will have the feeling 'why not me?' There are emotions that will well up inside them.

So then, you have a tendency at times, when you are telling the story about your trip, to dampen it down. People ask, 'how was your trip?' and you say, 'oh, it was good, the weather was great,' rather than, 'it was life changing,' and, 'we had such a delightful time!' There is a difference in the vibration.

This is what to do with your writing—do not dampen it down—continue to look at it from a lens of everything that happens is good for you.

You must tell the truth of what it was like for yourself. Let the dirty laundry hang out to yourself—and then you go back and read it, and maybe you decide later to take parts out.

But for now, there is nothing there to impede you. There is no voice on your shoulder saying 'do not say that,' or, 'it was not like that,' or, 'do not say it that way.'

If you cannot tell the truth of both sides, you will be keeping part of the picture out for yourself.

Be honest with your self. Take a 'truth serum'.

Talk about what happened at the time of the experience: when you were out east, and you walked into the door of this home of your aunt's that you were staying at, and you saw the cherry pits that your girls spit on the floor, what was your experience? You were mortified: that was a true and real experience for you.

In the moment, it was a true expression of mortification. It was a true expression in juxtaposition with other experiences of sheer delight. You were mortified, but you understood that you needed to teach your girls to respect others' things. If you walked in and didn't say anything, it wouldn't have been true to yourself.

You want to teach your children to honour and respect others. But without having that indicator of mortification, you would not have been able to understand the importance of teaching your children how it benefits them when they are out in the world.

This is the important thing to tell yourself, and to be at peace with. When you tell the truth, you can be at peace with how you responded rather than beating yourself up.

This is the freedom that needs to be passed on—in the final product of what you are writing.

Put the pieces of the puzzle out on the table and when all the pieces are there, depending on the picture you want to create, those are the pieces you will add.

This journey has been exciting for you with all its trials, and delights. The final picture will be the picture that you will hold in your own heart.

The final picture will be the one that you will take to bring joy in your life.

You react and respond to everything that happens in your life. You take a look at the experience. First you need to see it, but then you can go back and re-live it. Then, you can take away all the angst and you can look at it from the eyes of the joy of the experience.

All the tension is taken away.

All the angst that was there goes away and you are able to see clearly whatever the final gem was. You are more able to bring forth the joy—right at the beginning—when you are reliving the experience.

There is no more of the mortification, or the loud noises, or any aspect of what you were regretting in the moment. It was as simple as 'I saw something, and I was able to do this.'

You are capturing it in a softer way.

When you are in the midst of the experience, you are filled with fear. But all of it, the fear included, propelled you forward for change. This was the positive aspect of the experience. You don't discount it. You don't soften it for others. You just tell the truth to yourself. 'When this happened, I was broken. I was completely broken. But that was then and this is now, because out of it came this...'

Do you see?

And if you can all do this, if you are all able to honour your humanity and your reactions, but at the same time recognize that all of these experiences create the deliciousness and full-ness of life, how joyful would it be?

For the end product of every part of the journey is what you take away from each of these experiences.

How did you process it? Was it in such a way that you were able to 'accept' what it was, to be at peace with it, to come to peace with what it is, and to move forward?

This is the important message for you to be teaching and helping others with rather than looking at 'what am I doing right and wrong.'

Would it not be of benefit to you if you could look upon the scenery of something you enjoy—the ocean, with the calm waters, and the sunshine and the blue sky, and the fluffy clouds, and the beautiful warm breeze? You look at all of this and think, 'Wow, this is absolutely beautiful. And I am at peace with this. I like this.'

Would it not be good if you could look at that same scene when there is the dark sky, and the sea is brewing, and there is the cold breeze, and say, 'I am at peace with this. I can put on a coat. I can go inside. I am ok with this, and all is well.'

When there are the storms that glow, and the homes that are destroyed, and the people who perhaps have lost a loved one, it serves them well to have someone sit quietly with them and simply hold their hand and not try to change the scenery.

Let them be at peace with who they are. There is no need to change anything. Let everything be and let it flow. Learn to move with ease through the changes that life will bring.

For in truth, nothing changes. You are always in the presence of light. You are always with divinity. It is always the same.

The gist of all of this is please do not limit yourself: be honest and open with yourself and let *you* be your only audience at this point. When you look back, you will know intuitively what to include. Just keep writing.

Express the joy that you are experiencing with those who are close to you. Fear not as you write—they will lift you up and propel you forward. You will all rejoice for you have all walked the journey together.

For you are all helping each other write your own books of this life.

You are doing very well. You are one who is capable of doing this and you are doing it freely. Just don't fret too much about the final product.

You know this.

You know when you are flowing and in the deliciousness of it. There is just the pure flow of the joy—it is the pure flow of the God energy and the flow of the light.

And because you have that experience, you know when you are doing this, and when you are not. The knowledge of when you are doing this, gives you the contrast to know when you are not.

And, there is no need to doubt this whole experience. For it would not have been put upon your heart if you did not have the skills to complete it, my dear.

You cannot be another person. You must be Terri-Lynn.

God speaks to each one of you differently; the connection one has with divinity varies. There is just a need for you to trust it. There is not one better than the other. Each one of you is unique—it is the sharing with one another that allows you to share the connection that you have, and the true oneness of all of you.

Inspiration is inspiration; it is the breathing in of the air from source energy. This is something each one of you would say is the similarity.

Although the way you are able to interpret it and explain it to another may differ, it is all one and the same. The flow of energy is the same; the lamp just might be different. And that is what gives life its beauty.

And each one is very important and precious in the grand scheme of things. When you all on this earth expand, grow, and get closer in your ability to express the light, you create something totally magnificent.

You are all one and the same.

It is when you share with one another that you are expanding your view. That is it—it is nothing more than that. Sometimes you will have different definitions for the experience, but when you share with one another and you are talking, each one of you knows that you are working with the same light.

When you are writing quietly on your own and you are feeling those words flow through you, it is the exact same thing as someone who allows the formation of the words to come through their spoken voice. For you it is flowing through your hands, for the other one it comes through the voice.

It is the same energy, but just a different modality. It is nothing more than that.

Each one uses their own implement of choice.

At this time, this is what works for you, and this is what makes it exciting.

But the source energy is the same for each of you.

The inspiration, the intuitive notion, the ability to write what is flowing freely from God—it is all one and the same.

Let it flow, dear ones—all of you. Let it flow.

You ask, 'am I doing this right?' But your question in itself has a flaw because it is focusing on the *how it is coming through* versus the knowledge that *it is the light coming through.*

Let it keep coming.

Each one of you adds a piece to the puzzle.

And the sharing touches another in the soft places that they, too, need to be touched to gain clarity—and the end result is clearer.

And the life of the reader becomes enriched.

And that is why it is important. And why it is so valuable.

Many books you have read were written by people who had the flow coming through uncertainly, but they just kept writing.

And before you know it, you have that piece that you alone were able to bring forth; something that only you could give birth to. You were all instruments through which the information came, and you were the one who was chosen to write it down.

It belongs to no one, and it belongs to everyone.

Each one of you has a gift to bring to the world. For some it is a book, for others it is a song, or the birth of a child.

For others, it is as simple as reaching out a hand and showing compassion. These are the spiritual gifts that you are all given, along with the free will to extend it or not[11]. There is no judgment in that, it is simply a matter of choice.

When you are writing freely, none of these questions come up in your mind. Be encouraged to keep writing from that place, the place that fills the cells of your body with the light of the Lord.

And you come away feeling uplifted.

Do you not come away feeling fulfilled when you have stopped writing and you know you are done for the day?

Continue along this vein.

The questions that come later in your mind, just note them, but do not let them drag you down. Trust yourself dear one, that you have been given this project because it is yours. You have been chosen to do this work. You have been chosen to do the work that comes into your life.

Just note the tension and be at peace with it.

All is well.

ALL is well, dear one.

Embrace the joy within your own heart.

And the words will stop here, at this place.

But it is certainly not farewell.

There is so much being said within these pages to soften the path for you and for others.

They are speaking to your soul.

Listen.

Maybe Even More
(Final Thoughts)

*There will always be that feeling
that something is missing*

I have read these words countless times.

The book was first for me, after all. And, despite all of my listening, and remembering, I still have moments when I need to remember again.

Just yesterday, I almost fell into the trap of old belief systems; I had blocked the entire day to write, but had a deadline to finish a 'simple' on-line certification for a competitive sport that my children are in. The training took much longer than I expected; rather than the two hours I had set aside in the early morning to do it, it took me close to six hours to complete. And as the hours went by, grumbly monsters started emerging in my mind because I wasn't getting to my writing. Those old thoughts of, 'see, you're not so smart after all,' and 'why can't you get this?' and 'this shouldn't be taking you so long,' creeped into my mind.

But I stopped them in their tracks.

I acknowledged them, but I was not prepared to let them stay for too long.

I had to shower them with love, so I took a break.

Indeed, thoughts like these will still pop up from time to time—there is no reason why I should think that they wouldn't. But it's a matter of how quickly I notice it, acknowledge it, and then snap out of it that matters.

I'm never going to reach a state of perfection, and that's ok.

It's like my house: the purge of the rooms that I didn't get to in the first round finally got completed. And it felt good. Like the cobwebs in my mind that were cleared away over the year, the house's shadowy corners were also finally being cared for. But the act of cleaning, organizing, and purging every crook and cranny of the house still didn't make everything *perfect*. There were still things—here and there—that I wanted to make just so. And it's still not there yet.

So, I am learning to shift my focus. I am working on staying centred on the peaceful place that is found in the breath, in the connection, in the light, in the now.

But there will always be that feeling that something is missing, or needing fixing.

There will always be the temptation to reach for more: we never want to settle for less.

Sometimes this is our intuition speaking; it drives us forward toward positive change. It is the still small voice speaking.

But other times, it is a grumbly monster that beckons us to spiral into lower vibrational thinking, get stuck in the past, or make assumptions about ourselves that are lies.

And we may believe these untruths.

Looking back now, I think I may have been ashamed of my imperfections. Perhaps—I thought—by keeping myself busy, I limited my exposure, and this quality-not-quantity approach worked to prevent people from seeing all my flaws.

Perhaps—I felt—if they saw these imperfections, they wouldn't love me anymore.

And then I was home—all the time—and I was fully exposed. My family saw my flaws—front line—and they didn't turn me away. They loved me all the same.

Maybe even more.

What exposed me even further was that we had a relative staying with us during the time that much of this was written. His mere presence amplified the 'rawness' of the situation. It poked at me. It taunted me. With pure lack of intention, he was a mirror that reflected back to me the things I didn't want to see.

And all the things I definitely didn't want other people to see.

This could have distracted me away from the writing—but it ended up being a catalyst: it brought me closer to my thoughts, and more open to the wisdom.

It was the same with my husband. He was not the 'bad guy'. Unaware of the role he was playing, he also mirrored back to me all of the things that I—myself—needed to sort out.

This whole thing was all about the change needed in me. It wasn't about my husband. It wasn't about my kids. It was all about me.

And they loved me through the entire process.

And these words finally found their way out of my heart and into the world.

Their purpose is to bring love into this world, by being a catalyst for change. They serve to shine light into one's inner world: a world that can sometimes have some dark, shadowy places.

A world of difference starts with you.

It is my hope that you find solace in these words in times of darkness.

It is also my hope that the process that I went through to learn how to listen, and how to stay connected, inspires you to do the same.

We each have a power inside of us. A divine spirit that is available to each of us. It connects us to a higher wisdom.

We can access it at any moment, if we just choose to do so, when we take moments of stillness.

Many of the things I speak about in the book have worked to bring me to a better place of love, and happiness, and peace.

And now, I share it with you.

If anything I speak of resonates, learn more about it.

Yoga. Meditation: taking moments of silence and stillness. Journaling: asking bold questions, 'scripting out' the answers. Purging. Listening to your intuition. Being selective of what you read, watch, and listen to. Being mindful of the little things: blessing the glass of water before you drink it; taking a walk in the fresh air; thanking the grass that grows beneath your feet; wrapping yourself up in a warm blanket; showing gratitude for your cozy pillow. Reminding yourself that you are deserving of great things. Forgiving yourself and others...

There is a mountain of truth in all of this.

And we climb the mountain step by step.

We hear of many people who have had spiritual awakenings and have found their way far down the path of love and light. And the stories are glorious.

The question is how to pave the path to get there.

This is a personal account of how I made my way toward that place. But there is not one way that is better than the other.

Each of us is unique in our own way.

So draw your curtains back. Be proud of your light, for it is yours, and it has been given to you.

Know that there is no need for striving. There is no need to pave the path. You just have to follow the breadcrumbs. And it starts with the simplest thing: we listen.

Be guided by your counsel.[45]

Gratitude and Thankfulness

All of you—the hands and feet of God

I cannot emphasize enough the whirlwind of emotions I feel as to how all of this came together. It has reinforced to me—and helped me to embrace the fact—that things are constantly at play in our lives that are higher, bigger, and better than we can comprehend, if we choose to go along for the ride.

First and foremost, I start with voicing my gratitude and thankfulness for being chosen for such a divine-led journey, and for everything I learned—for how I grew—along the way.

It's like planting a garden: the harvester puts the seed in soil, and waters it when the clouds don't open naturally. But, the harvester can certainly not take claim for the creation of the seed in the first place. They merely do their part, knowing that there are higher powers at play that are beyond their control.

The dream—and the prayer—of putting pen to paper had been sealed away in my heart and forgotten about. It lay dormant, like in the dark days of winter, until various 'keys'— slowly but surely—unlocked, unleashed, unchained my heart and that little seed of a dream started sprouting...

I cannot express enough my love and appreciation to so many of these 'keys', the ones I call my 'cloud of witnesses':

First, to Diana Sanita who planted the seed of possibility in me to write a book—years and years ago—and wouldn't let go of reminding me that I had it in me. You have more strength and courage than anyone else I know. You are an inspiration to me and I am forever grateful for our friendship; to Melanie Groves—my tea-time friend who created space for me to embrace my inexplicable desire of 'going to the moon when people around me were thinking Bobcaygeon'. I will never tire of our deep, tear-filled conversations until the day I die; to Sharon McQueen—my out-east-road-trip friend—who has had an undeniable soul-kinship with me from the moment we met. Portions of this book would not exist if it were not for our countless discussions, where our intertwined-true-selves spoke to each other. Your love, your wisdom, and your heart fill me with joy like my Nanny always did...

Yes, let's pause to rewind the clock for a minute.

To my Mom (Noreen McMahon), who stood against many odds—and hours of labour—to give me a chance in this world. Your selfless act of love planted a drive in me to live a life of meaning, purpose, and significance. For this, I am eternally grateful; to my Dad (Tom McMahon) who took me under his wing and taught me the value of hard work—and helped me to understand that most people have soft hearts if you look hard enough; to my Aunt Marly (Cooper) who has always been there for me as a consummate encourager—you are my 'big sister' that helped me learn that there is healing in tears-through-laughter emotions. Always know that you are so loved just as you are; to my dear Aunt Heather (Baker) who gave me a place of refuge, and held a special place for me in her heart—may you rest in peace; to my 6'6" cousin who still lets me call him Little Larry

(Cooper). You call me your rock, and 'Nanny number two', but never underestimate what your tender heart is meant to do in this world, and the difference you make in mine.

To my Nanny (Madeline Cooper) who, from the moment she set eyes on me, seemed to have the lifelong purpose of lifting me up and filling me with love overflowing. She watered the seeds of my soul. As I live and breathe, I have never felt more loved by anyone in this world. I would be delighted beyond measure if even an ounce of her loving character and steadfast faith has rubbed off on me; and to my Grandma (Doris Runchey), whose love for quilting—and making-memories from them—inspired me to do the same for my girls.

And now to my immediate family...

To my husband—'Gareth Ledger and Edward in between'— you were an answered prayer to Queen's "Send me Someone to Love"[46] that I sung at the top of my lungs before I met you. Thank you for the adventurous 22+ years of marriage. May we always be reminded of the love we have for one another, of the beauty in our yin-yang nature, and that we can achieve anything when we work together.

And to my darling girls, Naomi and Desi: may you come to fully understand one day how much you are loved, and how much light you bring to my heart. You both bring out the little child in me. Naomi, you hold your old-soul personality with confidence. You dance to your own tune. You let your light and inner beauty sparkle for all to see. Always keep shining bright in faith and in love. Desi, you have such a heart of compassion for others (and animals) that comes through in everything you do. Your zest for life—and your laugh—is contagious. Your spontaneous proclamations like, 'I love life!' continue to bring joy and happiness. Never forget the trueness of who you are. You are both miracles that came to me in different ways—that reshaped my heart—and I am eternally thankful for the blessing of being your Mama.

Let's rewind the clock back again:

To Lynn Marie Landry—a 'kindred spirit' from our high school days—for opening your heart and home to me always, for even hitchhiking to come see me, and for believing in me when I didn't believe in myself—I am ever grateful; to Fernando Vitorino: our friendship has stood the test of time and circumstance and you have shown your love to me in so many selfless ways. No matter how much time passes, I am so thankful that we still stay young through each other's eyes.

To my cousin, Crystal Stere, for the ever-so-many special childhood memories we shared. Thank you for embracing me as I was, and for always making me feel worthy of love. You taught me how to share my heart, even if it took me a while to learn; to my godmother Ann McLeod, for lovingly filling up my hope chest—both literally and figuratively; to my brother Shannon (McMahon), and my sisters Erin (Leroux) and Alicia (McMahon), for loving me despite my black sheep tendencies and for letting me kiss and hug you every visit just in case it is the last; and to the Murray clan—thank you for the smiles and open arms, and giving me a sense of belonging: it means more than you know.

And now, more recently: to my yoga sisters, the Wednesday morning breakfast ladies (#frannie), the drama team, and the Wellington Square crew, thank you for your prayers, your encouragement, and your examples of unwavering faith.

To the remarkable women and men who graciously read earlier versions of this book: Diana Sanita, Melanie Groves, Suzanne Nagy, Gareth Ledger, Noreen McMahon (my Mom), Drew Maxwell, Sharon McQueen, Larry Cooper, Marilyn Cooper, Jen Kranjc, Nina Gorgani, Renita Persaud, Sam Lee

Loy, Stephanie Cooper, and Lindsay Reynolds. Each of you—in different ways, sometimes in mysterious ways, but always in beautiful ways—gave me your wisdom, courage, and glimpses into your heart. For your time, for your feedback, for your support, I am forever indebted to each of you.

On my publishing journey, the entire Friesen Press team has been spectacular. And, a special shout out to my editor: Cathy, your feedback on my manuscript blessed my heart and meant more to me than you will ever know.

And to the books and authors who have walked with me along my journeys in this life. I have learned from you, been shaped by you, and felt connection and belonging through your words.

All of you—the hands and feet of God—made up the fertile ground, the nutrients, the water, the sun, the foundation, and the roots that gently pushed this sprouted-seed-of-a-dream out of the ground; out of my heart and onto paper.

You kept me grounded. You kept me showered in love.

You helped this grow.

For we are all helping each other write our own books of this life...

Endnotes

1 Berstein, L. (1983). *I love you song*. On *Piggybank Songs: New Songs Sung to the Tune of Childhood Favourites*. Warren Publishing House.

2 Loes, H. D. (1920). Words from This Little Light of Mine.

3 Woolston, C. H., Barlowe, J., & Root, G. F. (1913). Jesus Loves the Little Children.

4 Joncas, M., & Ferguson, E. E. (1979). On Eagle's Wings [Vinyl]. North American Liturgy Resources.

5 Dufford, B. (1972). Be Not Afraid [Recorded by John Michael Talbot]. On Table of Plenty [CD]. The Orchard Music. (1997).

6 Schutte, D., Young, O., Armstrong, A., & Ferguson, J. A. (2001). Here I Am, Lord. OCP Publications

7 Ferguson, S. (2006). Big Girls Don't Cry. A&M Records.

8 Webber, A. L. (1997). You must love me: Don't cry for me Argentina: from the Cinergi motion Picture Evita. MCA Music Publishing

9 Rzeznik, J. (1998). Iris [Recorded by the Goo Goo Dolls]. On Dizzy Up The Girl [CD]. Burbank, CA: Warner Brothers Records.

10 Lennox, A. (1992). Why. On Diva. RCA Arista.

11 Adkins, A., Kurstin, G. (2015). Hello. Recorded by Adele, 25. Columbia.

12 Platten, R. (2015). Fight song. Columbia

13 Matthews, A. (2004). Reaching. Shake-a-Paw Music.

14 Collins, P. (1989). All of my Life. On But Seriously [Vinyl]. UK. Virgin.

15 Caillat, C., Babyface, & Carlsson, J. (2014). Try. On Gypsy heart [CD].
   Republic Records

16 Johnson, J., Nakamura, D., & Huston, P. (2005). Breakdown. On In
   Between Dreams {CD]. Brushfire.

17 Aguilera, C., Storch, S., & Morris, M., (2002). Walk Away. On Stripped
   {CD]. RCA.

18 Mitchell, J. (1971). River [Recorded by Sarah McLachlan]. On Wintersong
   [CD]. Nettwerk. (2006)

19 Smith, G. (1968). Come by the Hills [Recorded by Loreena McKennitt].
   On Elemental [CD]. Quinlan Road. (1985)

20 Phillips, W. (1990). Hold on. SBK Records.

21 Serbert, K. (2017). Rainbow. On Rainbow [CD]. Kemosabe &
   RCA Records.

22 McCain, E. (1998). I'll be. On Misguided Roses. Lava.

23 Garrett, S., Ballard, G. (1987). Man in the Mirror [Recorded by Michael
   Jackson]. On Bad [CD]. Epic Records.

24 Nicks, S. (1975). Landslide [Recorded by Dixie Chicks] on Home.
   Monument & Columbia Records. (2002).

25 Lennon, J., & McCartney, P. (1968). Blackbird. [Recorded by Sarah
   McLachlan]. On I am Sam [film soundtrack]. V2 Records. (2001).

26 Dawkins III, E. N. "Aloe Blacc"., Berling, T "Avicii"., Quinn, A., Marantz,
   M.M., McHugh, J., Einziger, M., (2013). Wake Me Up. On True. PRMD.

27 McLachlan, S., Egan, S., & Merenda, D. (1995). I Will Remember You.
   Artista Records, Incorporated.

28 Barlowe, C., Lindsey, H., Stevens, S. (2010). American Honey. On Need
   You Now [CD]. Capitol Nashville.

29 Aguilella, R., Haefeli, I., Tonra, E. (2011). Medicine. [Recorded by
   Daughter]. On The Wild Youth EP. Glassnote.

30 Jones, H. (1985). Life in One Day. On Dream into Action.
   WEA (Warner-Elekra-Atlantic).

31 Luke 6:38

32 Galatians 5:22-23

33 Philippians 4:8; Galatians 5:22; Proverbs 8:6

34 John 14:27

35 Sheeran, E. (2011). Autumn Leaves. On + (Plus). Asylum Records & Atlantic Records.

36 Blum, S. (2009). Waiting for Autumn (pp. 143). Hay House, Inc., Carlsbad, CA.

37 Philippians 4:5

38 Philippians 4:7

39 Matthew 18:22

40 Matthew 18:20

41 Petty, T. (1989). Free Fallin'. On Full Moon Fever [CD]. Wea Records.

42 2 Corinthians 5:8

43 Luke 23:34

44 1 Corinthians 12:7, 11; Galatians 5:13

45 Psalms 73:23-26

46 Mercury, F. (1973). Send Me Someone to Love. On A Day at The Races [Vinyl]. EMI Records Ltd.